Inclusive Classrooms
Video Cases on CD-ROM

Activity and Learning Guide

to accompany

The Inclusive Classroom:
Strategies for Effective Instruction
Second Edition
by
Margo A. Mastropieri and Thomas E. Scruggs

Prepared by
Anne M. Bauer, Professor
Stephen Kroeger, Gabbard Research Fellow
University of Cincinnati

PEARSON

Merrill
Prentice Hall

Upper Saddle River, New Jersey
Columbus, Ohio

10 9 8 7 6 5 4 3 2 1

ISBN: 0-13-039808-X

Contents

Part III: Resources

Acknowledgments

This project allowed us to observe teachers in action who were inspiring. Without their baring their souls and allowing us to observe their actions, these video cases and booklet could not have been produced. So, we gratefully acknowledge:

Sally Schmitt
Jane Chambers
Rog Lucido
Beth Kouche
Christine Hamm
Andrea Comarata
Cathy Burton

And their students and families.

Introduction

About the Cases

As you view these video cases, you will be seeing expert teachers in action. In the classroom cases, you will be watching classrooms in which children with learning disabilities, attention deficit disorders, and mild/moderate disabilities are successfully engaged in the classroom community and in learning. Because of the natural supports and inclusive stance of the teachers and schools, it may be difficult for you to identify which children are indeed identified as having disabilities or need of other accommodations.

As you view these cases, remember that these are expert teachers, and that no one begins his or her work in inclusive classrooms at this level of proficiency. However, you can practice the professional behaviors that they demonstrate. These teachers are not technicians; they are reflective professionals who are probably teaching their students very from the way in which you were taught. Just imagine how the very active children in the sixth-grade classroom would appear in a setting in which they were seated in rows copying notes from the overhead projector. What would their attention be like? How many of them would be putting forth their best effort? What if the children in the preschool classroom were to be "in seat" and "working" on workbook pages? Or if the physics teacher was standing at the podium lecturing from the book or having students take turns reading a paragraph from the text? What if the team members began their discussion of the troubled middle school student by listing problems rather than strengths, or began with the presumption that he did not fit and that there was a place for "students like him"?

Think back on your own experience as a student and recall a favorite teacher. What two or three core values did that teacher demonstrate? Do any of those values appear in these video cases? Can you articulate three important questions you have as a teacher? Are those questions answered here? How do these teachers view the children? Do they see the children as things to be fixed or are children approached as collaborators in a problem solving process? How do you perceive yourself as a team member? What do you do when you need assistance? Picture yourself in a video case; what practice would you be most excited about sharing with others? We hope this booklet will guide your reflection on the cases presented. Enter this process by asking questions and reflecting on your own experience.

In order to support your learning, we have provided several supports in this booklet. Each section begins with the Standards of the Council for Exceptional Children (CEC) that are addressed. In addition, we have cited the Interstate New Teacher Assessment and Support Consortium Standards (INTASC), adherence to which is required by many states. Reflections are included, as is an index, which cross-references all of the strategies for inclusion presented in the four cases on the CD-ROM. The key points of each case are then presented, followed by additional questions or guides for reflection. Sample responses to the questions are provided at the end of the booklet. We also include responses to "Frequently Asked Questions" about inclusive classrooms as well as references that may also be used for further reading on the wide range of topics we visit.

Watching expert teachers in inclusive settings makes it look easy. Remember the amount of planning it takes to have a menu of tasks available so that every student can be successful. Think about how exhausting it is to vigilantly monitoring young children and support your assistant teachers. Think about all of the details you must address in planning a field trip to a construction site. Think about the voices of these teachers, as they communicate their absolute belief that every child can learn, and should have the opportunity to shine. Enjoy seeing students actively engaged in learning. We enjoyed seeing these professionals in action, and hope you can find pieces of their work to use as you construct your own practice.

Using the CD-ROM

The video cases depicted on this CD-ROM show teachers engaged with students in various inclusive classroom settings employing strategies featured in the text. Each case has its own button on the navigation bar on the left of the screen. By clicking on the case of your choice, you move into the specific video clips and discussions of that case.

Video Clips
Each topic nine video clips. Individual clips are labeled according to the topics illustrated. Simply click on the thumbnail of one clip to watch the video segment. Across the bottom of the video screen you'll find buttons that allow you to pause, fast-forward, and rewind the clip.

Text Button
The text of the commentators for the CD-ROM is provided in this area, available for copying and pasting to your own study.

Internet Button
Clicking on the Internet button will allow you to select and mount an Internet browser such as Microsoft Explorer. Once an Internet browser is running you can visit the links provided, or insert an Internet address and go to literature sources, discussion groups, email, or other relevant sites.

Reflection Comments
When you highlight a specific video clip, comments concerning that clip become available. These comments help explain why selected video clips are interpreted as being examples of certain teaching or learning strategies for inclusion. The perspectives reveal the richness of meaning embedded in the living classroom when seen from the viewpoint of various stakeholders, including experts in the field, the teacher being observed, the

students involved, and the professional literature that provides the research base behind the teacher's decisions. Be sure to click on the arrow at the bottom that begins the audio.

Help Topics
The ? button provides a wealth of clear, step-by-step information. Clicking on the ? button will open up the help file, where you will find explanations and directions for every button, and a guided tour through using the CD and building your own study.

Click on a topic in the Help Topics Menu for a multimedia guide through each element in the CD, clarifying its navigation, purposes, and uses.

Click on Using the Study Builder, then Using Custom Studies for a complete guide through perhaps the most innovative and meaningful piece on the CD, the opportunity to build your own video cases, perfect for an electronic teaching portfolio.

Study Builder
To create your own study, begin by clicking on the Study Builder button on the navigation bar to the left.

Begin with your own question, then look for answers in the numerous video clips provided. For example, consider how to deal with the multiple intelligences of the learners within your classroom, or how to manage the class during group activities or small group instruction. Compare and contrast teaching and learning strategies for inclusion as they are applied with students at different age levels, in different schools around the country. Focus on these or any other question by isolating clips in which the instruction and strategies of the four cases supplies answers.

A total of eight clips can be used in each of your personal ethnographies. Isolate and sequence clips from the archived clips provided. Drag and drop your selected clips onto an open slot in the grid, then save and name your study. Now you're ready to finish by customizing your study under the Custom Studies button.

Step by Step Study Builder
1. Decide on a question.
2. Select clips that focus on that query.
3. Drag and drop the clips into the eight open slots.
4. Name the study.
5. Save the study.
6. Move on to the Custom Studies step.

For a more complete walk through this module, click on the help button, then on Study Builder under Help Topics.

Custom Study
Next, click on Custom Studies. Click on the name of your saved study in the Custom Studies field and add your own comments concerning each clip and the way it fits into

your study in the Custom Studies commentary. Or add selected commentary from the researchers and participants by clicking on Text on the navigation bar, choosing a category, and scrolling through the categorized transcripts. When you find the appropriate comments, simply highlight the section, use the edit button to copy the selection, and paste it into the commentary field on your custom study.

The Custom Studies tutorial found on the Help screen provides a helpful reminder, should you need a bit of assistance creating your study.

Step by Step Custom Study

1. Open the saved study.
2. Click on the chosen clip.
3. Add comments of your own, or pull comments from the text button.
4. When you've added all of your elements, save your study to your own hard drive or floppy disk.

Each custom study you create can be used to fulfill an assignment, or become part of your electronic teaching portfolio. Create as many custom studies as you like and examine your own understanding of any number of teaching strategies, techniques, and concerns.

Chapter 1:
What Are Inclusive Classrooms?

After completing this section, you will be able to:

- Describe assumptions made by teachers in inclusive settings
- Identify general considerations of inclusive classrooms
- Describe specific principles of inclusive settings

CEC Individualized General Curriculum Referenced Standards
Standard 1: Foundations
Knowledge: Principles of normalization and concept of least restrictive environment
Standard 3: Individual Learning Differences
Skill: Relate levels of support to the needs of the individual
Standard 5: Learning Environments and Social Interactions
Knowledge: Barriers to accessibility and acceptance of individuals with disabilities
Knowledge: Adaptation of the physical environment to provide optimal learning opportunities for individuals with disabilities
Knowledge: Methods of ensuring individual academic success in one-to-one, small-group, and large-group settings

CEC Individualized Independence Curriculum Referenced Standards
Standard 1: Foundations
Knowledge: Principles of normalization and concept of least restrictive environment
Standard 5: Learning Environments and Social Interactions
Knowledge: Barriers to accessibility and acceptance of individuals with disabilities
Knowledge: Adaptation of the physical environment to provide optimal learning opportunities for individuals with disabilities

INTASC Principle 9: The teacher is a reflective practitioner who continually evaluates the effects of his/her choices and actions on others (students, parents, and other professionals in the learning community) and who actively seeks out opportunities to grow professionally.

The New Experience of Inclusive Classrooms

Most preservice teachers bring to their program their own beliefs about teaching and learning. They may view educators as guides, friends, or confidants in the image of their favorite teacher rather than as professionals engaged in finding new meanings of teaching and learning (Calderhead, 1996). Yet the classroom in which you will be working will, in all probability, not resemble the classroom you attended in preschool, elementary school, or secondary school. You may have attended schools in which many of the students were much like you. You may not have been required to complete a large number of high-stakes assessments. The students with disabilities may have been educated in "that room down the hall." Everyone in your school may have had English as their first language.

As a teacher today, your life experiences may have been very different from those of the students with whom you are working. Jackson and Harper (2002) suggest that much has changed in classrooms in the last twenty to twenty-five years:

- There is increasing cultural, ethnic, and linguistic diversity.
- More students with disabilities are in general education classrooms.
- Special Education is seen as services rather than as a place to send children.
- Teacher, principals, and schools are held more accountable for the performance of students.

The changes in the classroom and in the climate of education make the teacher's job even more difficult. Beginning teachers are expected to be proficient in working in inclusive settings, and are often in "entry year" programs through which they may obtain a long-term license only after demonstrating some predetermined level of achievement on an assessment.

Reflection 1–1: Reflect on your own school experience. What was your first experience with individuals with diversity? How did you feel about that interaction? Do you think students today are having similar "first experiences"? Why or why not?

If inclusive classrooms are going to be successful, there must be changes in the traditional general education classroom of students in rows sitting quietly, reading, taking notes, and filling in worksheets. The old "special ed" model cannot be replicated; rather, the goal is to develop very good general education instruction (McCleskey & Waldron, 2001). This "very good" instruction will help every student in the classroom achieve to the best of his or her ability.

In their exploration of successful inclusive classrooms, McCleskey and Waldron (2002) asked teachers what needed to happen. Teachers reported that they felt students with disabilities could benefit from the classroom if two basic changes in classroom practice were made: (a) modifying the curriculum to enhance relevance for each student and (b) modifying instructional techniques. These modifications of instructional techniques, however, were often in keeping with what is generally characterized as good teaching. Teachers reported using more hands-on activities and fewer worksheets, more oral interaction and fewer paper-and-pencil tasks, more cooperative learning, reteaching of critical skills, and using supports (such as calculators) as students need them. How different, then are "good" inclusive classrooms from "good" classrooms in general?

Perhaps the most influential factor in the instructional setting is the teacher's knowledge and beliefs about teaching and learning (Lipson & Wixson, 1997). Teachers' beliefs shape the learning context (Schmidt, Rozendal, & Greenman, 2002). An essential assumption is that all children can learn and can be successful in the classroom. In McCleskey and Waldron's study, they reported that in inclusive classrooms expectations for all students were high, whereas in the past expectations for students had been too low. Students with disabilities would not have had the opportunity even to be exposed to much of the material presented in the classroom. In short, teachers in successful inclusive classrooms assume that every child should be there and that every child can be successful in the classroom. Teachers in inclusive settings assume that they are responsible for creating learning opportunities and removing barriers to learning and participation in their classrooms (Stanovich & Jordan, 2002).

Reflection 1–2: Lipson and Wixson (1997) suggest that the teacher's knowledge and beliefs about teaching and learning are the most influential factor in the success of inclusive classrooms. Select the Preschool, Sixth Grade, or High School case. What are some of the statements made by the teachers that communicate their beliefs about teaching and learning that could contribute to their success as teachers in inclusive settings?

General Considerations of Inclusive Settings

Even though each classroom has its own unique culture, composition, and characteristics, there are some general considerations in place in inclusive classrooms. These include reflective teachers, flexibility, individualization, caring, natural supports, and fairness.

Reflective teachers. Successful teachers in inclusive settings are more likely to seek help, and in doing so, more likely to expand their repertoire of teaching behaviors and collaboration. In inclusive settings, it is expected that teachers can't "go it alone" and meet the needs of everyone all by themselves. Rather, there are background players, including the principal, consultants, fellow teachers, parents, and related services personnel. These people can support the teacher and the child as well. Stanovich and Jordan (2002) describe successful teachers in inclusive classrooms as scientific practitioners, who observe their students, develop hypotheses about learning, develop plans, observe the results, and base further instruction on what they have learned. They seek answers to questions, and use people and resources to support their students' learning. In an inclusive classroom, teachers:

- Educate everyone in their classroom.
- Make decisions about instruction.
- Follow the general curriculum while making adaptations to help everyone succeed.
- Seek, use, and coordinate support for those who need extra help (Jenkins, Pious, & Jewell, 1990).

- The teacher is an enabler of students' learning and a partner with other professionals (Lipsky & Gartner, 1991).

Both the general educator's and special educator's roles and responsibilities shift in inclusive settings. Teachers are responsible to assess and accommodate individual academic, intellectual, and emotional needs. Special educators are facilitators and collaborators. Just as general educators may be challenged in learning new skills to meet the needs of students with disabilities, special educators may be unfamiliar with the general education structure and curriculum. Both general and special educators need to clarify their roles, responsibilities, and beliefs about the inclusion of students and disabilities, with a stance of purpose and commitment (Jackson, Harper, & Jackson, 2002).

Flexibility. Teachers in inclusive settings are effective at managing instructional time and have increased the engaged time of teaching and learning in their classrooms (Englert, Tarrant, & Mariage, 1991). They are flexible in grouping students, adapting activities, modifying their plans "on the fly," and utilize students and cooperative activities to free themselves up to address the needs of individual students   Flexibility allows interactions between teachers and students, between groups of students, and provides the opportunity to represent, participate, and be engaged within the social context of the classroom in many different ways (Jackson & Harper, 2002).

Individualization. In an inclusive setting you can't simply "teach to the middle." In their discussion of principles for alternate assessments, Ford, Davern, and Schnorr (2001) describe principles that clarify the general considerations of inclusive settings:

- *Priority should be given to the development of foundational skills.* These foundational skills include successfully interacting with people, gathering the needed information to complete a task or activity, solving problems, and contributing to the classroom. These are skills to be emphasized for all students, not just those with disabilities. We refer to these foundational skills as *keystone behaviors* because they are essential to the development of many other behaviors and to success in educational settings.

- *Good education implies individualization.* This doesn't mean every student in the classroom is doing something different. It means that the priorities for every student in the classroom may not be the same, and that the reason one student is participating in an activity may be different from the reason another is participating.

- *Everyone should have the opportunity to experience mastery and accomplishment.* Students should be able to feel as if they have finished something and finished it well. This means teachers can't simply "cover" a concept or topic, but must ensure that students have learned the information.

- *The quality of each student's educational experience is important.* Classrooms should not be joyless places in which activities are designed and implemented for students' "own good." The characteristics of moment-to-moment interactions among teachers and students should be positive. Ford, Davern, and Schnorr (2001) warn that the "task-oriented" view assumed by adults may create negative emotional responses in students or result in failing to take advantage of opportunities that may arise throughout the day.

Caring. In inclusive schools, the philosophy of caring and honoring and celebrating diversity is apparent. Cooperation reigns over competition, and each individual—teacher, principal, student, or parent—is an accepted participant in the community. No labels are given to students, classrooms, or teachers (Sapon-Shevin, 1990). Noddings (1984) suggested that when teachers care they are able to present reasons for their actions or inactions that would persuade an observer that they did what was best for the student.

Teachers' interactions with students influence students' perceptions of one another and their relationships (Montague & Rinaldi, 2001). In a study of teacher feedback and students' perceptions of their peers, White, Jones, and Sherman (1998) found that regardless of the target students' "reputation," negative teacher feedback caused the target child to be treated as less likable, less deserving of rewards, and more likely to be in trouble. The teacher's behavior affects the target student and his or her peers as well. Teacher interactions with students contribute to peer acceptance or rejection (Birch & Ladd, 1998). Caring, positive interactions are essential to inclusive classrooms.

Natural supports. It would be impossible for a teacher to meet every need of every child in his or her classroom. It would also interfere with the regular interactions in classrooms if instructional assistants did everything for students who vary from their peers. Natural supports are grounded in the belief that relying on the people who are usually in the environment increases the likelihood for success more than relying on specialized services and personnel (Nisbet, 1992). It is far less intrusive for a student to have the place in the book pointed out by a peer sitting next to him or her than for the teacher to swoop down and find the page. In a caring classroom, students begin to automatically pitch in when a peer needs support. These natural supports can include things like lending a peer a pencil, carrying his or her books, acting as scribe, making a carbon copy of notes, or writing down assignments.

Fairness. What is fair? Equal treatment or equal opportunity to succeed? Is it fair for students with learning disabilities to orally report information when other students are required to write it? The issue of fairness is often voiced by general education teachers (Jackson, Harper, & Jackson, 2002). In inclusive classrooms, individual changes for a student are not designed to reduce the load on the child. Rather, they are designed to reduce curricular barriers. If the barriers to accessing the curriculum are removed, then a level playing ground is available to all of the students. Chow, Blais, and Hemingway (1999) describe this as *equifinality*: in the end, all students have an equal opportunity to access education in an environment conducive to learning.

9

Specific Principles

There are several specific principles usually involved in the implementation of inclusion. These include natural proportion, normalization, and problem solving.

Natural proportion. The principle of natural proportion states that classrooms should reflect the characteristics of the community at large (Stainback & Stainback, 1991). There should be about the same number of boys, girls, students with disabilities, students who are gifted, creative or talented, or students from various ethnic, cultural, or language groups as you would find in the community surrounding the school. This is an ongoing challenge in inclusive classrooms in that sometimes more students with disabilities are assigned to teachers who are successful with them.

On the surface, implementing the principle of natural proportions seems simple. The composition of your classroom should look like the composition of the community. In reality, however, it is difficult to put in place. Principals tend to place students who are challenging with teachers who are successful in meeting those challenges. Word spreads through the parent communication network, and parents request teachers who do well with children who vary from their peers.

Normalization. *Normalization* means that a person with a disability should have the opportunity to live as similarly to others as possible (Nirje, 1967). Teachers must try to help students with disabilities have the same opportunities and experiences as their peers, although there may need to be adjustment. Some students may only be able to partially participate in an activity. Everyone is welcome at assemblies, presentations, and extracurricular activities. In one inclusive high school that we've studied, students with disabilities are included through the natural supports provided by their peers. Students who love athletics can participate through the spirit squad or through serving as "team managers" for example.

Solving an instructional problem rather than fixing a student problem. In special education, we have traditionally identified the child's problem and devised a way to mitigate that problem. In the problem-solving model, however, the reason for concern isn't within the child, but in a discrepancy between the learner's actual and expected performance. The traditional model focuses on student characteristics that must be changed and removed so that the student will no longer have the problem. In the problem-solving model, efforts are made to describe the context and identify ways to provide the supports to help the student be successful. The problem-solving model assumes that assessment, design, implementation, and reassessment occur in a recursive cycle throughout the student's educational career (Salvia & Ysseldyke, 1991).

The recursive cycle of assessment, design, implementation, and reassessment.
Assessment is incorporated into a the collaborative problem solving model, in which:

- the issue is identified.
- comprehensive information is collected to generate and explore hypotheses about the child's characteristics, environmental factors, and interactions between the child and the environment.
- a plan is devised.
- progress is monitored, with continuous assessment.

There has been a shift from fixing a student when the student doesn't fit the school or curriculum to fixing the curriculum and the school to meet the needs of all learners (Jackson & Harper, 2002).

Reflection 1–5: Think of a student whom you have observed who is struggling. Is he currently viewed as the problem? Is the emphasis on fixing the student or fixing the mismatch between the student and the setting?

Looking in Inclusive Settings

So, what will you be seeing in the inclusive settings in these video cases? You will be seeing classrooms and settings in which:

- it is sometimes difficult to identify which children do indeed have disabilities, because the strengths of each child are exploited;
- teachers have a commitment to meeting the needs of each child, care deeply about each child, and reflect on their instructional and managerial decisions about each student;
- individualization is an ongoing teaching process;
- the proportions of children with disabilities and from various cultural, ethnic, and language groups are similar to those found in the community at large;
- normalization is a goal for all students;

- the emphasis is on solving instructional problems rather than "fixing" students.

Welcome to inclusive classrooms!

Chapter 2:
Instructional Planning in Inclusive Classrooms

After completing this section, you will be able to:

- describe the application of Universal Design to inclusive classrooms.
- identify effective instructional practices for inclusive classrooms.
- implement differentiated instruction.

CEC Individualized General Curriculum Referenced Standards

Standard 3: Individual Learning Differences

Skill: Relate levels of support to the needs of the individual.

Standard 4: Instructional Strategies

Knowledge: Advantages and limitations of instructional strategies and practices for teaching individuals with disabilities

Knowledge: Strategies for integrating student-initiated learning experiences into ongoing instruction

Knowledge: Methods for guiding individuals in identifying and organizing critical content.

Skill: Use research-supported methods for academic and non-academic instruction of individuals with disabilities.

Skill: Modify pace of instruction and provide organizational cues.

Skill: Identify and teach basic structures and relationships within and across curricula.

Skill: Use instructional methods to strengthen and compensate for deficits in perception, comprehension, memory, and retrieval.

Skill: Use responses and errors to guide instructional decisions and provide feedback to learners.

Standard 5: Learning Environments and Social Interactions

Knowledge: Barriers to accessibility and acceptance of individuals with disabilities

Knowledge: Adaptation of the physical environment to provide optimal learning opportunities for individuals with disabilities

Knowledge: Methods of ensuring individual academic success in one-to-one, small-group, and large-group settings

Skill: Establish a consistent classroom routine for individuals with disabilities.

Standard 7: Instructional Planning

Knowledge: Integrate academic instruction and behavior management for individuals and groups with disabilities.

Skill: Select and use specialized instructional strategies appropriate to the abilities and needs of the individual.

Skill: Plan and implement age- and ability-appropriate instruction for individuals with disabilities.

Skill: Design, implement, and evaluate instructional programs that enhance social participation across environments.

CEC Individualized Independence Curriculum Referenced Standards
    Standard 3: Individual Learning Differences
        Skill: Relate levels of support to the needs of the individual
    Standard 4: Instructional Strategies
        Knowledge: Strategies for integrating student initiated learning
        experiences into ongoing instruction
        Skill: Use research-supported instructional strategies and practices.
        Skill: Identify and teach basic structures and relationships within and
        across curricula
    Standard 5: Learning Environments and Social Interactions
        Knowledge: Barriers to accessibility and acceptance of individuals with
        disabilities
        Knowledge: Adaptation of the physical environment to provide optimal
        learning opportunities for individuals with disabilities
        Knowledge: Methods of ensuring individual academic success in one-to-
        one, small-group, and large-group settings
    Standard 7: Instructional Planning
        Skill: Plan and implement age- and ability-appropriate instruction for
        individuals with disabilities.
        Skill: Design, implement, and evaluate instructional programs that
        enhance social participation across environments.

INTASC Principle 2: The teacher understands how children learn and develop, and can provide learning opportunities that support their intellectual, social, and personal development.

INTASC Principle 3: The teacher understands how students differ in their approaches to learning and creates instructional opportunities that are adapted to diverse learners.

INTASC Principle 4: The teacher understands and uses a variety of instructional strategies to encourage students' development of critical thinking, problem solving, and performance skills.

INTASC Principle 5: The teacher uses an understanding of individual and group motivation and behavior to create a learning environment that encourages positive social interaction, active engagement in learning, and self-motivation.

INTASC Principle 6: The teacher uses knowledge of effective verbal, nonverbal, and media communication techniques to foster active inquiry, collaboration, and supportive interaction in the classroom.

The key ingredient to effective teaching and learning for all students is instruction, not placement (Jackson, Harper, & Jackson, 2002). As we begin this discussion of instructional planning for students with disabilities, we are assuming that the greatest part of the instruction for students with disabilities occurs in the general education classroom. We are also assuming that the effective teaching strategies used to meet the needs of students with disabilities will enhance the instruction for all students in the classroom. The models we'll present include Universal Design, effective teaching, and differentiated instruction.

Universal Design

Since the Americans with Disabilities Act was passed in 1990, buildings have had to change in terms of their accessibility. The term *Universal Design* was coined by an architect who dreamed that new structures and spaces could be made accessible by design from the beginning (Mace, 1997). He argued that by placing accessibility on the table during the design phase, the cost of such changes would be reduced. Rather than retrofitting ramps after a building was constructed, architects, in their designs, included ways for people who use wheelchairs to enter the building. In addition, the modification helps more than individuals with disabilities. Pisha and Coyne (2001) provide the example of the curb cuts—the slopes built into sidewalks at intersections and crosswalks—that were designed to make it possible for individuals with wheelchairs to navigate more easily. Many people without identified disabilities use the curb cut, including parents with strollers, bicyclists, people pushing dollies, and individuals with carts. The inexpensive modification, now planned for all sidewalks, benefits many people. Although it originated in architecture, the concept of Universal Design has been applied to accessibility in learning.

In education, Universal Design is an effort to increase the likelihood that future curricula for all students will (a) be accessible, (c) be interactive, and (c) enable the progress of all students, whether or not they are identified as having disabilities (Jackson, Harper, & Jackson, 2002). In learning, Universal Design means that the design of instructional materials and activities allows individuals with wide differences in their abilities to see, hear, speak, move, read, write, pay attention, organize, engage, and remember to achieve in the classroom (Orkwis & McLane, 1998). Adaptations for students with learning disabilities are subtle and unobtrusive, and support more than those learners who are identified as having disabilities. Pisha and Coyne (2001) suggest that features of the Universal Design for Learning can be useful to many students and implemented in such a way that outcome for all learners may improve.

Universal Design for Learning opportunities functions on three guiding principles outlined by Rose and Meyer (2000):

- *Multiple, flexible methods of presentation are used to support diverse recognition networks for the students.* For example, depending on how students best recognize and use information, material may be presented orally, in images, as video, as a song, in Braille, or in a hands-on activity. A simple example of this principle occurs when a teacher verbally announces a page number, writes the page number on the board, and scans to make sure everyone is on the correct page, physically helping those who are not.

- *Multiple, flexible methods of expression and apprenticeships are used to support students' various strategic networks.* Students may construct a model, draw a picture, answer a multiple-choice quiz, write a letter, or take an essay test to demonstrate their knowledge or practice a skill. In the sixth-grade social studies video case, for example, students demonstrate their knowledge of ancient Egypt through constructing pyramids, writing newspaper articles, and drawing pictures.

- *Multiple, flexible options for engagement are used to support diverse affective networks.* Students would explore their own interests, or be provided the extrinsic as well as intrinsic motivational structures they need. Students are provided choices, and a specific attempt is made to interest students. For example, students may be provided a menu of activities from which they may choose, or examples may be provided from their own everyday lives.

Universal design goes beyond the content of a curriculum, to its goals, methods, and ways of assessing growth and learning. Orkwis and McLane (1998) provide a framework that summarizes the main principles of universal design for learning. The first principle, that of providing flexible means of representation, challenges teachers to develop alternatives that reduce perceptual barriers. Using text, audio, or images alone may create barriers for students. Using digital text, closed captioning, and images with verbal description circumvents these perceptual barriers. Cognitive barriers, if present, can be addressed through providing summaries of the "big ideas," improving access for some students and review for others. In addition, background knowledge may also be provided for students with limited experiences.

To ensure flexible means of expression—the second principle—teachers should consider individual differences in motor and cognitive skills. Alternatives to expression through writing, speaking, or drawing, may need to be provided to address motor barriers. In terms of cognitive barriers, making strategies explicit or conspicuous may be helpful. Rather than depending on their intuition, some children may need strategies to be taught explicitly, step-by-step. Scaffolding may also be helpful, providing temporary support for learning that is gradually reduced as the student becomes more confident.

Providing flexible means of engagement—the third principle— may also be a challenge. To help more students stay engaged, students should have flexibility in terms of the amount of support and challenge they receive. Flexible options should also be provided in terms of novelty and familiarity. For example, some students require a great deal of repetition, whereas others thrive on randomness, and surprise. Developmental and cultural interest should also be considered. Finally, curricular materials should be flexible enough so that each student can contribute to the curriculum by adding his or her own images, sounds, words, and texts. This flexibility leads to deeper engagement, allowing for direct input from students with differing abilities.

One application of Universal Design for Learning is the Strategic Reader Project (Pisha & Coyne, 2001). In this project, guidelines are proposed to increase the accessibility of the material in textbooks to students. These guidelines include:

- *Support the recognition of patterns.* In efforts to make textbooks attractive, publishers may make the layout "busy: and confusing to students. The Strategic Reader Project suggests providing a simplified and clarified presentation of the core content, without graphics and sidebars. In addition, it suggests an outline view of key topics for students.

- *Provide supports for the use of strategies.* The way a book is designed can support a student's use of strategies. Students can be provided with an outline first, which can serve as an advance organizer. The student can then be directed to read the chapter. Finally, students can be referred back to the outline to pinpoint major topics for tests. In addition, an easy way to look up unfamiliar concepts or terms must be provided.

- *Provide supports for engagement.* Levels of engagement have been found to be improved when students are able to use concept-mapping software and other strategies to aid organization of textbook information. Using authentic activities and projects with high relevance also increases students' engagement.

Reflection 2–1: Select one of your textbooks. Based on the three guidelines listed above, how accessible do you think it is?

We recognize that Universal Design is complex, and challenges instructional planning. Issues and concepts of Universal Design are presented in a visual display at the end of this section.

Effective Instructional Practices in Inclusive Classrooms

Jackson, Harper, and Jackson (2002) delineate several effective teaching methods for inclusive classrooms. These include:

- *Collaboration among stakeholders to shape and realize a positive, appropriate, learning environment.* Teachers involve the community, parents, and students. Students are partners in their own education rather than recipients. The over-riding question is, "How can we all work together so that everyone is successful?"

- *Parental involvement to maximize learning time, support students' learning, and provide for communication between home and school.* Parent involvement requires parent communication. Parents should understand what is happening in the classroom both academically and socially, and why. This goes beyond the typical parent newsletter, conference, or invitation to performances. The National Parent Teacher Association (1997) suggests (a) regular, meaningful *two-way* communication; (b) promoting and supporting parenting skills; (c) active parent participation in student learning; (d) welcoming parent volunteers; (e) including parents in decision making; and (f) outreach in the community for resources that can strengthen the educational experience.

- *A self-directed learning environment, in which students learn to set goals and engage in self-instruction and self-monitoring.* In a self-directed learning environment, students are encouraged to independently accomplish tasks and manage their own behavior. When students are not engaged in self-direction, they may develop learned helplessness. Learned helplessness (Weiss, 1981) is a sense that behavior is independent of outcomes. For example, a student who studies and consistently fails spelling tests may no longer bother to study the spelling list because of the perception that it doesn't matter—he always fails anyway.

- *Peer supports, so that learners can be both teachers and learners in the classroom, engaged in cooperative rather than competitive learning experiences.* Students helping students is far less intrusive than pulling out students to work with adult tutors. Students can encourage each other, act as "study buddies," or provide tutoring to each other.

- *Flexible grouping, allowing students to work in a variety of structures to meet their current needs and to construct social knowledge.* Not everyone works well independently, and not everyone works well in a group. In addition, even though we as adults recognize that we don't work well with some people and do work well with others, we assume that our students can work equally well with everyone. Mixing up the groups and grouping allows everyone a better chance of success socially and academically.

- *Both explicit and implicit instruction, in which children learn skills and are presented with open-ended and authentic learning opportunities.* Explicitness allows students to better understand expectations for performance as well as concepts being presented. However, only using explicit instruction fails to allow students to practice expressing and creating related to the content. Both explicit instruction and open-ended, real activities are needed.

- *Formative evaluation, measuring the results of instruction in authentic ways.* Most of the evaluation that occurs in classrooms is summative: students are judged on what they have learned, and then move on to something else. Formative evaluation helps students and teachers see what still needs to be learned. Applying the evaluation to real tasks increases the inherent value of the assessment to students.

These methods, although identified for students with disabilities, have a positive impact on the instruction of all students. As you review the video cases, you will have the opportunity to view these methods in action.

Initially presented in a discussion of including children in physical education activities, Block (1994) provides questions for the evaluation of instructional tactics in inclusive settings:

- Does the plan allow the students with disabilities to participate successfully, yet still be challenged? Are materials age-related?
- Does the plan have a negative impact on students without disabilities?
- Does the plan place undue burden on the teacher?

Reflection 2–2: One of Block's criteria is that the instructional tactic has no negative impact on students without disabilities. What sort of tactic would have a negative impact? If the teacher is following the Universal Design for Learning, is it possible that an instructional strategy would be harmful to other students?

Differentiated Instruction

Differentiated instruction recognizes that students vary in their background knowledge, readiness, language, preferences, interactions, and responses to instruction (Hall, 2002). In a differentiated classroom, teachers use a variety of (a) ways to explore the curriculum content; (b) sense making activities through which students can construct knowledge; and (c) options for students to demonstrate what they have learned (Tomlinson, 1995). Tomlinson (1995) suggests that four characteristics shape teaching and learning in differentiated classrooms:

1. *Instruction is focused on the concepts and driven by principles.* The goal isn't to "cover" material, but to make sure that each student has the opportunity to explore and apply the key concepts of the subject.

2. *Assessment of student readiness and growth are built into the curriculum.* Assessment is constant, with the teacher providing support when students need additional help, and extending exploration when the students are ready to move ahead.

3. *Students work in a variety of patterns.* Sometimes students work independently, sometimes in pairs, sometimes in groups.

4. *Students actively explore the content, and teachers guide that exploration.* The teacher is a facilitator of the varied activities that occur simultaneously. The student-centeredness increases students' ownership of their own learning and supports their developing independence.

There are three elements of the curriculum that teachers can differentiate. Tomlinson (2001) provides several guidelines for differentiating each of these elements:

Content: Differentiation requires that several elements and materials be used to support instructional content. These tasks must be aligned to learning goals. The instruction is concept-focused, and teachers must focus on the concepts, principles, and skills students need. For example, in the high school physics classroom, students are using outside resources, computers, and adapted materials. In the sixth-grade classroom, students are provided the opportunity to practice using a sledge in addition to having a verbal explanation.

Process: Flexible grouping is consistently used. In addition, classroom management benefits both students and teachers. Students may work in teams, independently, or in pairs. Grouping varies with the activity. Students may also be provided choice in how they will attack a task.

Products: Ongoing formal and informal assessments provide the teacher with information about students' readiness and growth. Students function as active and responsible explorers, with each child feeling challenged most of the time. Expectations and requirements vary for each student's responses. Students may self-select their products, or may be provided support in completing the activity they have chosen.

In addition to these three general curricular elements, Tomlinson provides several guidelines for practice. First, the teacher should clarify key concepts and generalizations to ensure that all students are learning. Assessment becomes a teaching tool to extend rather than to measure learning. Critical and creative thinking are goals in lesson design, requiring that students understand and apply meaning. All learners must be engaged, with a variety of tasks offered within instruction as well as across students. Finally, there should be a balance between teacher-assigned and student-selected tasks, ensuring that students have choices in their learning.

Differentiated instruction creates a flow in the classroom that you may not have experienced as a student. Tomlinson (1995) describes this flow in this way:

- The whole class begins to work on a topic or concept with a general presentation.
- Students then work independently, in pairs, or in small groups, using varied materials depending on their readiness and strengths, to further explore the topic or concept.
- The whole class comes together to share what they have learned and to develop questions.
- Students move back to specific tasks designed to help them make sense of key ideas at varied levels of complexity.
- The whole class comes together again, under the direction of the teacher, to review key ideas and share what they have learned.
- The teacher presents problems, cases, or activities that students then work on in small, student-selected groups.

- The whole class comes together for mini-lessons in the skills that will later be needed to make presentations about the teacher-generated problems, cases, or activities.
- Students self-select activities through which they will apply and extend their learning.
- The whole class comes together under the direction of the teacher to share individual study plans and establish how the products will be evaluated.

This ebb and flow has several strengths. Students are engaged, provided choices, and have built-in opportunities to move about the room. The teacher has the opportunity to view students working with other students and demonstrating what they know about the concept.

Reflection 2–3: Review your own experience as a student. In what ways have teachers used assessment as a teaching tool? How has it been used to measure your learning? Give examples of each.

Instructional planning in inclusive classrooms is a complex task. However, teachers often feel more comfortable in terms of instruction than they do in terms of classroom management. In the next section, we will explore managing inclusive classrooms.

Universal Design – Three Essential Qualities

Universal design attempts to create a curriculum without adaptation or retrofitting by providing equal access to information. Universal design allows the student to control the method of accessing information. The teacher monitors the process and initiates new methods. Through Universal design, the teacher encourages students' self-sufficiency, and imparts knowledge and facilitates learning. Universal design does not remove challenges—it removes barriers to access. There are three essential qualities of universal design.

1. Representation:	2. Engagement:	3. Expression:
Course content offers various methods of representation. Universally designed content provides alternative representations of essential concepts. Various methods of representation can allow the student to learn the information in their preferred means. (Example: notes placed on Web)	Course content offers various methods of engagement. Universally designed course content maintains various skill levels, preferences, and interests by allowing for options. By having flexible teaching strategies and course content, students can choose methods that support their interest and skill levels. (Example: appropriate reading level options)	Course content offers various methods of expression. Universally designed course content allows for alternative methods of expression, giving the student multiple means of demonstrating mastery of the material. (Examples: oral, written, fine motor, alternate formats)

Implementation:

- Place course content on-line
- Use peer mentoring, group discussion, cooperative learning
- Use guided notes to get at essential concepts (avoid copying notes from overhead)
- Update materials based on current events and student demands
- Provide comprehensive syllabus—clear requirements, accommodations and due dates

- Develop study guides
- Gives frequent tests that are shorter in length
- fluctuate instruction (seven intelligences)
- Clarify, ask for questions, repeat and given additional examples
- Relate a new topic to one already learned
- Tape record lessons with copy of notes
- Allow demonstration of knowledge through alternative means
- Encourage use of adaptive technology

TERM: Architect M. Bednar (1977) noted that the functional capacity of all people is enhanced when environmental barriers are removed. The term *accessible design* was used in the early 1980s to describe the value of universal design, but accessible has become synonymous with making environments usable primarily by people with disabilities, losing its more inclusive connotation of making environments understandable and usable by all people.

An accessible building means much more than having a wheelchair ramp. Is the building convenient to public transportation?

Is the front door easily located? Does it provide good directories? Finding one's way is usually not part of the image of accessibility, but it is an essential feature of universal design. Approach to a problem is integrative rather than by separate committee. Universal design attempts to eliminate the "we-they" dichotomy. The passage of the Americans with Disabilities Act (1990) heralded the possibility of a paradigm shift in thinking, moving the discussion from building codes to civil rights. Moreover, it requires life-span thinking.
(*Strategies for Teaching Universal Design*, P. Welch, 1995)

The Principles of Universal Design
Design of products and environments to be usable by all people, to the greatest extent possible, without the need for adaptation or specialist design

ONE: Equitable Use	TWO: Flexible Use	THREE: Simple & Intuitive Use
The design is useful and marketable to people with diverse abilities	The design accommodates a wide range of individual preferences and abilities	Use of the design is easy to understand, regardless of experience, knowledge, language skills, or concentration level
Guidelines:	Guidelines:	Guidelines:
1a. Provide same means of use for all: identical whenever possible, equivalent when not	2a. Provide choices in methods of use	3a. Eliminate unnecessary complexity
1b. Avoid segregating or stigmatizing	2b. Accommodate right-/left-handed access	3b. Consistent with user expectations and intuition
1c. Provide for privacy, security and safety of all	2c. Facilitate user accuracy and precision	3c. Accommodate range of literacy/language skills
1d. Make the design appealing to all	2d. Provide adaptability to user pace	3d. Arrange information according to importance
		3e. Provide effective prompting/feedback during and after task completion

FOUR: Perceptible Information	FIVE: Tolerance for Error	SIX: Low Physical Effort	SEVEN: Size and Space
The design communicates necessary information effectively, regardless of ambient conditions or the user's sensory abilities.	The design minimizes hazards and the adverse consequences of accidental or unintended actions.	The design can be used efficiently and comfortable and with a minimum of fatigue.	Appropriate size and space is provided for approach, reach, manipulation, and use, regardless of user's body size, posture, or mobility.
Guidelines:	Guidelines:	Guidelines:	Guidelines:
4a. Use different modes (pictorial, verbal, tactile) for redundant presentation of essential information	5a. Arrange elements to minimize hazards and errors: most-used elements, most accessible; hazardous elements eliminated, isolated or shielded.	6a. Allow user to maintain a neutral body position	7a. Provide a clear line of sight to important elements for any seated or standing user
4b. Provide adequate contrast between essential information and nonessential information	5b. Provide warnings of hazards and errors	6b. Use reasonable operating forces	7b. Make reach to all components comfortable for any seated or standing user
4c. Maximize "legibility" of essential information	5c. Provide fail safe features	6c. Minimize repetitive actions	7c. Accommodate variations in hand and grip size
4d. Differentiate elements in ways that can be described (i.e., easy to give instructions or directions)	5d. Discourage unconscious action in tasks that require vigilance	6d. Minimize sustained physical effort	7d. Provide adequate space for the use of assertive devices or personal assistance
4e. Provide compatibility with a variety of techniques or devices used by people with sensory limitations			

USABLE Design address by principles. Also, consider economic, engineering, cultural, gender, and environmental considerations in the design process.
Copyright material 1997 NC State University, The Center for Universal Design.

Differentiated Instruction

National Center on Accessing the General Curriculum
U.S. Office of Special Education Program: Ideas That Work

We are unique and the classroom is diverse. Differentiated instruction approaches learning so that students have multiple options for acquiring information and making sense of ideas. Differentiated learning requires flexibility, variety and adjustment of curriculum and delivery to learners in contrast to the expectation that students modify themselves for the curriculum. The flexibility of instruction in the classroom uses a blend of whole group, group, and individual instruction.

In one classroom, students express diversity in terms of background knowledge, readiness and language, preferences in learning, interests, and responsiveness. The goal of a differentiated learning procedure would be to maximize each student's growth and individual success. The process assesses learners where they are and builds instruction from there. Content, process, and products are three key elements of differentiation (Tomlinson, 2001).

Content	Process	Products
Several elements and materials are used to support instructional content	Flexible grouping is consistently used	Initial and on-going assessment of student readiness and growth are essential
Includes: acts, concepts, generalizations or principles, attitudes, and skills. The variation seen in a differentiated classroom is most frequently the manner in which students gain access to important learning. Access to the content is key.	Expectations are there to work together as students develop knowledge of new content. Whole class intro discussions about big ideas followed by small group or pair work. Grouping is not fixed. Grouping and regrouping is a foundation of differentiated instruction.	Pre-assessment leads to functional differentiation. Assessments include: interviews, surveys, performance, formal procedures. Assessment informs teachers to develop a menu of approaches, choices, scaffolds for varying needs, interests and abilities.
Align tasks and objects to learning goals	Classroom management benefits students and teachers	Students are active and responsible explorers
High-stakes tests and incremental steps of skill building tasks. Objectives-driven menu makes it easier to find the next instructional step for learners entering at varying levels.	Consider organization and instructional delivery strategies to operate a classroom.	Each task placed before the learner will be interesting, engaging and accessible to essential understanding and skills. Each child feels challenged most of the time.
Instruction is concept-focused and principle driven	**GUIDELINES** Making differentiation possible • Clarify key concepts and generalization • Use assessment as a teaching tool to extend versus merely measure instruction. • Emphasize critical and creative thinking: understand & apply • Engaging all learners is essential: task variation • Provide a balance between teacher-assisted and student-selected tasks	Vary expectations and requirements for student responses
Concepts are broad based and not focused on minute details or unlimited facts. Teachers focus on the concepts, principles, and skills students should learn. Complexity is adjusted for diversity.		Items that students respond to are differentiated to demonstrate knowledge and understanding. Varied means of expression, procedure and difficulty, types of evaluation scoring

Graphic organized by S. Kroeger, 2002

Chapter 3:
Managing Behavior in Inclusive Classrooms

After completing this section, you will be able to:

- describe how teachers manage behavior day to day
- describe assumptions made by teachers about managing behavior
- identify general considerations of behavior management
- describe specific principles and tools of behavior management

CEC Individualized General Curriculum Referenced Standards
Standard 1: Foundations
Knowledge: Principles of normalization and concept of least restrictive environment
Knowledge: Theory of reinforcement techniques in serving individuals with disabilities
Knowledge: Theories of behavior problems of individuals with disabilities
Standard 2: Development and Characteristics of Learners
Knowledge: Psychological and social-emotional characteristics of individuals with disabilities
Standard 3: Individual Learning Differences
Knowledge: Impact of multiple disabilities on behavior
Skill: Relate levels of support to the needs of the individual
Standard 4: Instructional Strategies
Knowledge: Prevention and intervention strategies for individuals with disabilities
Knowledge: Strategies for integrating student-initiated learning experiences into ongoing instruction
Skill: Use research-supported instructional strategies and practices
Skill: Use a variety of non-aversive techniques to control targeted behaviors and maintain attention of individuals with disabilities
Standard 5: Learning Environments and Social Interactions
Knowledge: Barriers to accessibility and acceptance of individuals with disabilities
Knowledge: Adaptation of the physical environment to provide optimal learning opportunities for individuals with disabilities
Knowledge: Methods of ensuring individual academic success in one-to-one, small-group, and large-group settings
Skill: Use skills in problem solving and conflict resolution
Standard 8: Assessment
Skill: Implement procedures for assessing and reporting both appropriate and problematic social behaviors of individuals with disabilities
Skill: Select, adapt, and modify assessments to accommodate the unique abilities and needs of individuals with disabilities
Skill: Monitor intragroup behavior change across subjects and activities

INTASC Principle 5: The teacher uses an understanding of individual and group motivation and behavior to create a learning environment that encourages positive social interaction, active engagement in learning, and self-motivation.

INTASC Principle 9: The teacher is a reflective practitioner who continually evaluates the effects of his/her choices and actions on others (students, parents, and other professionals in the learning community) and who actively seeks out opportunities to grow professionally.

INTASC Principle 10: The teacher fosters relationships with school colleagues, parents, and agencies in the larger community to support students' learning and well-being.

Managing Classrooms Day to Day

Managing classrooms is not based on interventions; rather it is grounded in classroom climate and effective instructional practices. Good and Brophy (1995) identified several attributes of teachers who encourage positive interactions in their classrooms. These teachers are:

- cheerful, friendly, mature, and sincere
- self-confident and calm in a crisis
- good listeners who are able to avoid win/lose conflicts and who maintain a problem-solving orientation
- realistic in their perceptions of themselves and their students
- able to enjoy their students while remaining in the role of teacher
- clear and comfortable about their role as teacher
- patient and determined in working with students who continue to test limits
- accepting of individual students but perhaps not their behavior
- firm yet flexible.

Teachers often consider classroom management a greater challenge than instruction. They are concerned about appearances and making sure that they are perceived by others as "in charge" in the classroom. However, as Redl (1959) suggests, teachers don't always have to react to student behavior. A teacher may permit, tolerate, interfere, or prevent behaviors from occurring. For example, if a student doesn't have something he needs for an activity, the teacher may permit him or her to return to his desk to get it. The teacher may also tolerate it, however, allowing the student to go but giving him or her a "teacher look" to communicate that it may be fine this time, but it isn't the desired behavior. The teacher may also interfere, using what Long, Morse, and Newman (1980) refer to as surface management techniques. The teacher may also prevent the behavior from occurring, by giving the students reminders to get all of their materials and not beginning the activity until everyone shows him or her that they have what they need.

These surface techniques are the ways in which teachers manage student behavior day to day. They include:
- *Planned ignoring* – the teacher simply ignores the behavior.

- *Signal interference* – the teacher provides the student with a nonverbal gesture or cue that the behavior is inappropriate. Signals are useful because usually they don't interfere with the ongoing activity. The "teacher look" falls into this category.

- *Proximity control* – the teacher moves forward or stands near the student who is engaged or appears to about to engage in problem behavior.

- *Interest boosting* – the teacher encourages a student to continue a task either by increasing interest in the task or in the student's efforts at the task

- *Humor* – the teacher uses humor to decrease tension or anxiety. Humor is never directed at a student or a group.

- *Hurdle helping* – the teacher provides help to the student before he or she begins to have a problem, reacting to an increase in tension, anxiety, or frustration.

- *Restructuring the program* – good teachers know when to abandon or adapt a lesson or activity that is falling apart rather than continuing to plunge onward.

- *Support from routine* – routines provide structure and security to students, and reduce the cognitive complexity of the classroom.

- *Appeal to values* – the teacher appeals to the students' understanding of fairness, authority, and the consequences of their behavior on themselves and others.

- *Removing seductive objects* – the teacher may remove an object that is distracting to or disturbing the student with the understanding that it will be returned at the appropriate time.

- *Antiseptic bouncing* – the teacher asks the student to go to another place so that he or she can calm down or regain self-control. The teacher communicates to the student that he or she is not being punished, but rather needs a break to continue.

Reflection 3–1: Think about your observations in classrooms or your own experience as a teacher. Describe an example when each of these surface management techniques was used.

Sometimes behaviors are such that surface management tools are not adequate. In these situations, Daniels (1998) suggests that teachers ask themselves the following questions:

- Could this behavior be a result of what or how I am teaching? Is the content too difficult or too easy? Should I try another instructional strategy?

- Could this behavior be the result of the students' inability to understand what I am teaching? Students may demonstrate undesirable behaviors when they are not ready for the material being presented, when they are frustrated, or when the activity has no meaning to them.

- Could the behavior be related to the student's disability? For example, if a student avoids reading out loud, maybe he or she is unable to read fluently and embarrassed.

- Could the behavior be a result of the arrangement of the room? Sitting in desks in rows for 50 minutes with little opportunity for movement is difficult for all students.

- Could the behavior be related to things you cannot control? For example, if a student has a difficult or long ride on the bus every morning, it may be difficult to transition to class work.

- Could the behavior be related to your class routines? Are routines so complex that students have a difficult time managing them?

Understanding Behaviors in a Larger Context

The inclusive classroom is a more complex learning environment than classrooms of twenty years ago. Teachers report that behavior management is an area of critical need, but receives little attention in their professional preparation. Teachers often find themselves feeling confused and seeking immediate solutions to complex behaviors. Lunchroom advice and anecdotal approaches may not address the larger needs of students in the classroom. Furthermore, we may be used to approaching students with problem behaviors with a "fix it" mentality, thinking that if we had the correct technique the problem would go away.

Aptner and Propper (1986) suggest that there is no magical answer. We need to think of problem behavior in terms of a troubled system and see the student in a reciprocal context of interaction with the environment. Aptner and Propper outline a rationale for thinking ecologically. First, past efforts may have failed because the focus may have been too narrow. Second, the child is seldom, if ever, the whole problem. Third, every one in the child's environment has needs; pay attention to all of them. Fourth, close attention to relationships and linkages may be the single most important determinant of success. Finally, the impact of an ecological approach can go beyond the child.

Bronfenbrenner (1986) describes various nested systems in which the individual's development takes place. For example, consider the relationship of the person to him- or herself. In addition, there are one-to-one relationships, interactions among settings in the context of community, work and school, all of which are set in a particular culture and society. Each one of these relationships influences the individual's development. Frequently perception of a child's behavior is appropriate in one setting, and seen as entirely inappropriate in another setting. This incongruence, or mismatch, is a point of imbalance (Apter & Propper, 1986). Incongruence is a disparity between the individual's abilities and the demands or expectations of the environment. In inclusive settings, the emphasis is on addressing this mismatch rather than fixing the child.

The systems approach sees the child as an inseparable part of a social system. An intervention is the process of helping maintain balance between the individual and the environment in three major areas. Not only do we look for changes in the child, but we also change the environment, which includes the attitudes and expectations for this individual. This systems approach to understanding behavior requires a teacher to step back and think through and about his or her environment. It requires specificity. In other words, as teachers we take time to examine our practice. We carefully consider the content of our teaching, as well as how we deliver the content.

The principle of reflective action can be traced as far back as Dewey (1933). Unlike routine action, reflective action requires the active, persistent, and careful consideration of any belief or form of knowledge in terms of its consequences and the grounds that support it (Zeichner, 1987).

Zeichner and Liston (1987) discuss Van Manen's conception of "levels of reflectivity." The first level is called technical rationality. It is concerned mainly with efficient application of educational knowledge for the purposes of attaining ends that are accepted as given and not treated as problematic. Many teachers find themselves in this technical level of reflection. Learning the skills of the profession require knowledge of how to present a lesson and gaining a clear understanding of the content.

Practical action is the second level of reflection. Practical action deal with explaining and clarifying the assumptions and predispositions underlying practical affairs, and assessing the educational consequences towards which action leads. Each action is linked to particular value commitments, and the actor considers the worth of competing ends. The teacher must step back from events and actions and enter a discourse with him- or herself. Practical action explores alternate ways and methods of explaining.

The third level of reflection—critical reflection—includes emphasis from the other two levels. It also incorporates moral and ethical criteria into the discourse about practical action. Which of our goals leads toward a form of life mediated by concerns for justice, equity, and concrete fulfillment? Do current arrangements serve human purposes and needs?

Educators find time to reflect on their professional practice in order to improve it. The reflective action cycle deepens our sense of ownership and responsibility for our profession. We no longer simply transmit information from one place to another. We understand the content knowledge, where it came from, and how it influences our world. Such a reflective teacher brings this same level of inquiry to situations and behaviors that are challenging.

Reflection 3–2: Look back on your own experience when you might have been "in trouble." Can you identify various factors that may have influenced your behaviors? What other systems were involved? How did you find your way through? What kind of support system surrounded you?

System-wide Support

School-wide structures can support students with learning disabilities and emotional-behavioral disorders. The Amendments to the Individuals with Disabilities Education Act (IDEA, 1997) require the use of positive behavior support when students' behavior impedes learning. Examining a specific problematic behavior can be helpful, but it is important to examine any behavior in the context of the larger environment. Whereas traditional problem solving has emphasized the examination of the consequences and reinforcers of behavior, positive behavior support tends to learn from all the factors involved in a behavior.

Positive Behavior Support has several assumptions.

- *Behavior serves a function or a purpose for the individual.* Behaviors do not occur "out of the blue" but are meaningful for the individual. A student may forget his or her book repeatedly if he or she is unable to understand the content.

- *Intervention is instructional and preventive.* Interventions address antecedent procedures, social skills training, consequence procedures, as well as curricular adaptations. The idea is to teach the student the appropriate ways to interact and to prevent the development of more severe problems.

- *Interventions are based on individual needs.* Needs are assessed across various environments through various means such as observations that are both formal and informal. There is no one way, for example to deal with talking out, missing homework, or inattention. Rather, the ways of addressing each behavior depend on the student.

- *Interventions are comprehensive and consider long-term outcomes over the span of years.* While we try to change behaviors in a short-term context, we do so with long-term outcomes in mind. There are no quick fixes, and each behavior is considered important. For example, the decision to reduce the number of spelling words for a student is weighed in terms of the long-term impact of reducing demands.

Sugai and Horner (1994) have outlined a number of critical components that school staff considers for system-wide change. There is a need for clearly defined expectations and consequences. Students need to know what is expected, and what will occur if they do not meet those expectations. In addition, teachers should make an effort to teach and acknowledge appropriate social behavior. Dangerous situations must be responded to rapidly, with help for all individuals involved, including observers. All members of the school community should monitor behavior and give feedback to staff.

Turnbull and associates (2002) describe positive behavior support as a broad range of systematic and individualized strategies for achieving important social and learning outcomes while preventing problem behavior. It is a data-based proactive decision-making and problem-solving process. Positive behavior support emphasizes a quality of life focus in natural settings. A key focus of positive behavior support is a process of building responsive environments that work over time in favor of appropriate student behavior and preferred quality of life outcomes.

There are three levels of positive behavior support. First, universal support considers the entire school and community context of the behaviors of all students. Second, group support considers difficult behaviors in increasingly smaller numbers. Third, individual support focuses attention on individual behaviors and uses functional behavioral assessment as its primary tool of analysis.

At the level of universal support, Turnbull and associates (2002) describe five key processes:

- Clearly define three to five universal behavioral expectations in simple, succinct, and positive ways. (For example: be safe, be cooperative, be ready to learn, be respectful, and be responsible.)

- Explicitly teach expectations so that all students know exactly what is expected of them. (A teacher is nominated to meet with each "unit" of the school to identify generic instructional needs and setting.)

- Extensively communicate the universal expectations on a school-wide basis. (Teachers and students develop codes of conduct around the five universal expectations. Use lesson plans to teach these directly in the classroom. Lesson plan includes: introduction, rationale, descriptions of setting of instruction, list of non-exemplars and exemplars, opportunity to practice and receive feedback, awarding achievement, public recognition.)

- Comprehensively implement a school-wide positive reinforcement system. (Use a ticket system in which winners are announced daily and given a tangible award, display photos and expectations in the hallway.)

- Evaluate progress through a team process and make adaptations based on data. (Does it increase positive interaction? Is there a sense of accomplishment? Are students in special education equally included?)

At the level of group support, administrators and teachers provide positive behavior support in the largest unit that is feasible for the particular students in need of more intense attention. The goal of an assessment is to determine the patterns of appropriate and inappropriate behavior among groups of students.

The level of individual support is typically provided to students with disabilities who have problem behaviors. IDEA talks about behaviors that impede one's own learning or the learning of others. Positive behavior support has been proven effective. At the heart of individual support is the functional behavioral assessment.

Reflection 3–3: What does it mean to be a change agent in a learning environment? What are the dispositions of staff members who demonstrate a willingness to learn and change practice for the good of the learner?

Functional Behavioral Assessment

IDEA `97 requires that a Functional Behavioral Assessment be conducted for a student either before or not later than 10 days after a disciplinary action (615.k.1.B.1). Functional behavioral assessment provides a structured procedure to "re-see" not only the student and the behavior of concern, but also the biological, social, affective, and environmental factors that initiate, maintain, or end the behavior in question. Functional behavior assessment helps teachers and families create a collaborative context to examine behaviors. This encourages a focus on problem solving around student growth.

There are four assumptions of functional behavioral assessment:

- Every behavior serves a function for the individual

- Behavioral interventions are most effective when they teach the individual what to do instead of what not to do.

- Interventions are more effective when they work many people in many places

- Only use a procedure with an individual identified with a disability that you would use with an individual not identified with a disability. (Bambara & Mitchell-Kvacky, 1994).

At the heart of the functional behavioral assessment is the development of a clear picture of the individual in all of his or her different settings. A set of questions form the steps of the process.

- Who should be on the team?
- What information do we need to make good decisions?
- How will we gather the information?
- What is the target behavior?
- What hypothesis explains the situation?
- What are our measurable goals?
- How can we help the person reach these goals?
- How will we monitor intervention effectiveness?
- Is it working?
- What are the next steps?

Once a team has worked together through a functional behavioral assessment, they begin to view their teaching environment differently. The functional behavioral assessment is rooted in a problem-solving view of the child. The process influences perspective and assumptions about behavior management.

Setting Events

Setting events are occurrences in a student's life that alter the value of different reinforcers and thereby change the impact that typical stimuli (i.e., teacher praise) have on the student's behaviors. In other words, the situation is larger than the immediate antecedents and consequences in a particular situation (Dadson & Horner, 1993). We tend to approach reinforcers as having a stable value when in fact they are not stable, but change according to other pre-existing conditions (Horner, Vaughn, Day, & Ard, 1996).

Effective behavioral interventions typically involve changing existing environments in a way that makes problem behaviors irrelevant, ineffective, and inefficient (Horner, 1996). Lack of sleep may alter the effectiveness of social interaction. If a child was recently in an argument, the next classroom may get the brunt of his or her anger. An effective intervention could be to introduce a less difficult task before assigning the challenging task.

Kennedy and Itkonen (1993) distinguish between concurrent setting events and preceding setting events. Concurrent setting events occur at the same times as the behavior. For example, a child may demonstrate a problem behavior during an instructional task. Preceding setting events are those that occur prior to the demonstration of the problem behavior. On days when Anita woke up late and slept on the her way to school, she also missed her breakfast. This led to a significant increase in problem behaviors on those days. Interventions involved waking up on time and eating a healthy breakfast. Setting events often occur outside the school day. Interventions may need to be considered at these times as well. Collaboration with families and others outside the school environment may be required.

Positive Behavior Support

Bishop and Jubala (1995) describe positive behavior support as having an important agenda. Is it not enough simply to eliminate the presence of target behaviors. We must provide students with increased access to skills and means of meeting needs in an appropriate and effective manner. With some adaptations, the following is a behavior plan presented by Bishop and Jubala (1995).

Behavior Support Plan
- Plan developed for: Jamshid
- Developed by: Jamshid's father, Ms. Newbury (fifth-grade teacher), Mrs. Priest (special education support teacher), Mr. Shirai (classroom aide), Ms. Chavez (vice principal)
- Date of plan approval: July 27, 1994
- Description of target behavior: Jamshid will squeal at a loud sharp pitch then hit and/or push his peer without disabilities during academic periods of the day.
- Functional assessment findings: Anecdotal records indicate the behavior is most likely to occur during academic activities, whether during individual work or cooperative groups. Adapted scatter plot reveals behavior occurs near the end of teach activity period. A specific S-R-C chart indicates that the trigger appear to be peers attempting to collect his work, build upon his work, or edit his work.
- Hypothesis and test information: Last year in his special day class, many of the tasks Jamshid completed were given to another group to sort into recycling bins or to take apart to be reused as an activity the following day. The function of Jamshid's behavior seems to be to protect his tangible work from destruction. This was tested by allowing Jamshid to keep his own work after completing it individually or within groups. On those days, Jamshid did not hit or push peers.
- Lifestyle enhancements: Maintain his full inclusion with same peers. At home Jamshid will be given his own toy chest to keep his things separate from those of his siblings and to share when he wants to.
- Environmental changes: Jamshid will be allowed initially to put his completed work in a folder in his desk to be checked by the teacher and returned to the folder after school each day. Jamshid will be allowed to collect work from others throughout the day and will return checked work to others. The next step will be for him to collect his own work and turn it in with the other students' work, at which time the aide will check it and return it to him immediately. In cooperative work groups, he will participate in reporting by holding up or pointing to his contribution to the project. He will be allowed to keep the product at his desk as soon as the group is over and then after a 10-minute period he will be assisted in

taking the project to the work display table with the other group projects. This will eventually be faded to the same procedure the rest of the class follows.

- Specific positive procedures: Not necessary. However, the reinforcement inventory suggests that Jamshid likes to look at books in the reading corner, likes orange soda, and likes playing with toy figures such as space creatures.
- Alternate behaviors and instructional strategies: Jamshid will be taught to improve his interactions with peers by increasing the number and type of symbols in his communication wallet. Existing symbols consist of objects and people he is interested in. New symbols will represent request, denials, and feelings. New symbols will be taught by systematically pairing symbol use with teacher verbalization of the symbol and peer support by immediately responding to the interaction. Specific instructional strategies will be delineated on an attached sheet.
- Crisis management procedures: If Jamshid squeals, he is likely to follow with hitting or punching a peer. Should Jamshid begin to squeal, an adult will quickly intervene by physically standing between Jamshid and the peer and facilitating Jamshid's communication, asking peers to respond. Should Jamshid follow through with a hit or a push, the adult will deflect the attempt with his or her arm and follow through with communication symbols.

The collaborative problem solving approach to difficult behaviors helps create a hopeful environment. The student and parent/guardian are critical members of the team. While there are no magical or easy answers, the collaborative process is more effective and more child-centered. In the next section, we will consider issues related to working as a team.

Reflection 3–5: Consider a situation in which you have worked or observed a student with challenging behaviors. What would be your description of the student from a teacher-centered point of view? How would you describe the behavior from a student-centered, problem-solving point of view?

Chapter 4:
Collaborating to Meet the Needs of Students

After completing this section, you will be able to:

- Describe assumptions made by teachers about collaboration
- Identify general considerations of collaboration
- Describe specific principles and tools of collaboration

CEC Individualized General Curriculum Referenced Standards
Standard 1: Foundations
Knowledge: Principles of normalization and concept of least restrictive environment
Standard 4: Instructional Strategies
Knowledge: Resources and techniques used to transition individuals with disabilities into and out of school and post-school environments
Knowledge: Strategies for integrating student-initiated learning experiences into ongoing instruction
Standard 5: Learning Environments and Social Interactions
Knowledge: Barriers to accessibility and acceptance of individuals with disabilities
Knowledge: Adaptation of the physical environment to provide optimal learning opportunities for individuals with disabilities
Standard 8: Assessment
Skill: Select, adapt and modify assessments to accommodate the unique abilities and needs of individuals with disabilities
Standard 9: Professional and Ethical Practice
Skill: Seek information regarding protocols, procedural guidelines, and policies designed to assist individuals with disabilities as they participate in school- and community-based activities
Standard 10: Collaboration
Knowledge: Parent education programs and behavior management guides that address severe behavior problems and facilitate communication for individuals with disabilities

INTASC Principle 5: The teacher uses an understanding of individual and group motivation and behavior to create a learning environment that encourages positive social interaction, active engagement in learning, and self-motivation.

INTASC Principle 6: The teacher uses knowledge of effective verbal, nonverbal, and media communication techniques to foster active inquiry, collaboration, and supportive interaction in the classroom.

INTASC Principle 9: The teacher is a reflective practitioner who continually evaluates the effects of his/her choices and actions on others (students, parents, and other professionals in the learning community) and who actively seeks out opportunities to grow professionally.

INTASC Principle 10: The teacher fosters relationships with school colleagues, parents, and agencies in the larger community to support students' learning and well-being.

Collaboration in the Classroom

Classrooms have traditionally been isolated from a collaborative problem-solving approach. The metaphor of the school as an egg carton illustrates the nature of this isolation (Lortie, 1975). While classrooms are situated side by side, how often do we collaborate with one another in planning and instruction? In fact, Lortie explains that when teachers do ask for help or assistance, it is often perceived as a lack of competence. We sink or swim alone. Hoy and Woolfolk (1990) suggest that during the socialization of teachers, what works in the short run is the major criterion. With the principal looking in classrooms, controlling students becomes an end in itself. Kagen (1992) points out that this need for control is something of an obsession for beginning teachers. Teachers need to engage a process of reconceptualization that allows them to move through stages of fantasy, survival, mastery and impact.

Collaborative problem solving is inquiry-based reflection. Gore and Zeichner (1991) describe three types of reflection embedded in teaching practice. First, technical reflection centers around a concern for efficacy and effectiveness of the use of teaching practices. Second, practical reflection explains and clarifies assumptions and predispositions underlying one's actions, and assesses the educational goals of an activity. Third, critical reflection uses explicit moral and ethical criteria to assess practical action in terms of where our actions are taking us. Are they, for example leading us towards justice, equity, caring, and compassion? The role of the teacher is engagement in a multitude of partnerships that use reflection on all three levels.

Reflection 4–1: Can you think of a particular situation in which you were required to use all three levels of reflection? What were the technical aspects of the problem? What were the assumptions and predispositions involved in the goals of the activity or situation? What values guided the process? What ethical concerns were embedded in the situation? Were values in conflict?

General Considerations of Collaboration

Partnerships. The discussion of Universal Design, Differentiated Learning Strategies, and Positive Behavior Support all assume a collaborative teaching stance. These systems assume a teaching stance of partnerships working to meet the needs of students. Promoting and facilitating student competence is a core component of teaching. Teachers collaborate to establish student needs, make referrals, and determine placement. Special educators form collaborative partnerships with general educators to create appropriate adaptations and modifications. Collaborative partnerships are required with paraprofessionals, parents and families, and the larger community.

Critical reflection is fundamental to understanding the significant levels of diversity involved in partnerships of collaboration. Any given environment will present different perceptions of needs and priorities. The competence of the child and effective practice to support competence is the context in which we consider and reflect on this diversity. Guild (1994) explains five components that are important to consider in order to avoid making naïve inferences. These components include:

- *Students of any particular age will differ in the ways in which they learn.* Students may need to read information, hear it, practice it, act it out, verbally rehearse it, use manipulatives, or apply it to a problem in order to learn.

- *Learning styles are a function of both nature and nurture.* Students don't learn the way we do simply because of our biology or because of how we have been taught, but as a result of the interaction of these two aspects of their development.

- *Learning styles, in themselves, are neither good nor bad.* Even though schools tend to emphasize verbal, sequential tasks, there is nothing wrong with being a visual, kinesthetic, or auditory learner.

- *Within any group, the variations among individuals are as great as their commonalities.* It is impossible to describe the typical student.

- *There is cultural conflict between some students and the typical learning experience in school.* For example, a Latino student who culturally functions in a collaborative family may have difficulty with a majority culture teacher's judgment that he or she cheated on an assignment because he or she received help.

Consistent with the systems perspective, collaborative action involves using a wide variety of interactions to understand, assess and problem-solve any particular situation. The Executive Committee of the Council for Children with Behavior Disorders (1989) recommends a functional and nonbiased assessment of learners from diverse backgrounds. For example, the focus should be on the classroom and school learning environments. The cultures and expectations of the learner, teacher and administrator should all be considered. Effective and efficient instructional procedures must be in place.

Collaboration with partners in all the systems is important, but a critical partnership is the one teachers form with students. Rogers, Waller, and Perrin (1987) refer to this partnership as "facilitated learning," which is characterized by extended conversations with the students. These conversations provide teachers with access to student cognitive processes and have less emphasis on controlling behavior. Working in collaborative relationships allows teachers to share a meaningful level of empathy with their students. Rather than taking more and more control of the classroom, teachers are slowly teaching students to take control of their own learning process. In the collaborative process, students are taught to co-create learning processes and classroom management rules, rather than be controlled by them.

Teacher/Student Assistance Teams

Hayek (1987) defines teacher/student assistance teams as teacher-centered support systems. The goal is to develop ways in which the teacher or teaching team can better meet students' needs.

Team initiation and formation depend on the situation. Frequently a teacher or several teachers see that a student is struggling. The teacher may have already begun a series of interventions and had several conversations with a parent. When the problem persists, the teacher or parent asks for assistance. Many teams will enlist broad participation. A general and special educator, an administrator, the school counselor and school psychologist, the school nurse, parents, and social workers are all considered potential team members. Teacher/Student Assistance Teams may already have an assigned leader and coordinator.

The initial activities of the team involve seeking a clear picture of the situation. The team will determine what they need to do in order to gather data that will help create this picture. Consistent with a systems approach the team will look at the entire environment where the student is present. Curriculum content, delivery styles, classroom arrangements, times of the day, and social and physical needs are all considered when planning observations and interviews. Staff development and training may be included in the process.

A simple process guides team procedures during a meeting: define the problem, develop a plan, and design a way to monitor and evaluate the progress of the student. Facilitation skills are important in this process to avoid the temptation to become stuck in any one phase of the process. For example, when defining the problem, a team needs to move towards a clear definition and not get bogged down with too much repetitive description. During the meeting, the time should be carefully monitored to prompt the team to move through the entire process of problem solving in a timely fashion.

By the end of the meeting, the team will have produced a document that outlines the components of the intervention. The document should be clearly understandable to its intended audience—another teacher, parents, and so on. The document should outline the nature of the problem, what needs to happen to support the student, who is responsible for each aspect of the intervention, the monitoring procedure, and finally, the date on which the team will reconvene to evaluate and determine next steps.

When we consider the complexity of a normal school day for both teachers and students, it is easy to see some of the threats to an effective intervention. Making a commitment to the plan and evaluating it is important to the success of a plan. A plan may be well-designed, but if the specific components of the plan are not implemented consistently and for a long enough period of time, the plan might be judged as ineffective. With regular evaluation and monitoring points, team members are more likely to follow through, and the child more likely will benefit from the plan.

Principles and Tools of Collaboration

Collaboration is a difficult task, and is not always successful. Guiding principles of successful collaboration presented by Friend and Cook (1992) include:

- Collaboration is voluntary
- Collaboration requires parity between individuals
- Collaboration is grounded in mutual goals
- Collaboration depends on shared responsibility for participation and decision making
- Individuals who collaborate share their resources
- Individuals who collaborate share accountability for outcomes

    Emergent characteristics of collaboration include:

- Individuals who collaborate value the interpersonal nature of collaboration
- Professionals who collaborate trust one another
- A sense of community evolves from collaboration

Reflection 4–2: Consider a situation in which "collaboration" was allegedly taking place. What key principles were included? What were absent? How successful was the collaboration?

Role release. A key aspect of collaboration that is often difficult for teachers and specialists alike is that of role release. Role release, described by Lyon and Lyon (1980), identifies three levels of working together:

- All members of the team share general information about their individual expertise, duties, and responsibilities
- Individual team members support other team members to make specific teaching decisions within their own areas of expertise.
- Team members share the skills specific to their areas of expertise.

Role release addresses a problem that sometimes occurs during collaboration: turfism. The level of sharing and respect generated by role release is very helpful in working with students. For example, if you have a student who is receiving support from the communication specialist or speech pathologist, far less progress will be made if the only "therapy" he or she receives is in the 20 minutes twice a week during which the specialist can see the student one-on-one. In terms of assessment information, as a teacher you have important information about how the student communicates to peers and in the classroom. The communication specialist or speech pathologist can "release" to you some ways to encourage language and to help meet the students' objectives.

Communication. Collaboration requires strong communication skills. Pugach and Johnson (1995) suggest that there are several communication barriers that hinder collaboration. These include:

- *Giving advice.* Telling someone what he or she should do can have a negative effect on the professionalism and respect needed in a collaborative relationship.

- *Giving false reassurances.* It doesn't help to tell a team member he or she will be fine when he or she is not feeling that way.

- *Misdirected questions.* Getting off topic or asking tangential questions can take time away from the discussion and problem solving that needs to take place.

- *Inattention.* During any collaborative meeting, everyone needs to focus on the task at hand. Not paying attention to others' contribution can limit the outcome of the meeting.

- *Interruptions.* In addition to being rude, interruptions have an impact on the speakers thought processes and organizing comments.

- *Using clichés.* Resorting to clichés can diminish participation.

- *Moving too quickly to problem solving.* Collaboration takes much longer than solving the problem by yourself. But, the ownership and information gathered by collaboration is invaluable. Moving too quickly diminishes the contributions of the team members and may appear to minimize the problem.

As a contrast, Pugach and Johnson recommend using active listening skills and:

- Offering support
- Using general, nonthreatening openings.
- Restating what another individual contributed to make sure the information is clear.
- Verbalizing the message you feel is being implied.
- Asking the speaker to clarify.
- Allowing silence to occur so that participants can reflect.
- Putting events in the proper order and context.
- Summarizing so that everyone has an opportunity to agree or disagree with what was said.

As we continue to reconceptualize the teaching profession, collaboration is a keystone behavior that will characterize the daily operation of what we do as educators. In inclusive settings, collaboration is a key way of working. As you view the cases, consider the ways in which collaboration occurs.

Case 1: Preschool

Providing an inclusive environment for young children can be very complex. All young children are learning social and school behavior. When students have disabilities, a wide range of behaviors may be apparent in the classroom. In addition, these disabilities interact with setting events, cultural issues, and the language learning of young children.

Anticipation and redirection. Often the teacher can anticipate a student's behavior and interact with the child in such a way that enables the child to be more successful. Sometimes nudging a child in a different direction may be all that is needed.

Natural supports. The least intrusive supports are those that occur naturally in the environment. Peers are key. Even at a young age, peers can be helpful for students.

Materials/space. The instructional environment can be planned so that productive behavior is encouraged. The placement of materials can encourage positive behavior and discourage challenging behaviors.

Monitoring and evaluating. Teachers are constantly evaluating students' progress and their own interactions. They are always scanning the classroom, taking in interactions between adults and children alike.

Keystone behaviors. An important aspect of addressing challenging behaviors with young children is to look at a keystone behavior—a behavior that has a significant impact on the child's quality of life. In addition, it's important to use comprehensive interventions—interventions that can be employed throughout the day and address several of the child's needs at one time. For example, a keystone behavior would be turn taking. If a child is able to take turns, his quality of life is changed in terms of being able to converse, play a game, and get a drink from the water fountain. And if the intervention is to be near the child when such events occur, provide the rationale for the behavior, as well as a physical prompt, the intervention is comprehensive, addressing language and behavior simultaneously.

Collaboration. Young children can be puzzling. Working with the director, a fellow teacher, or a support person can be very helpful.

Structure and routines. Young children may come from environments that are less predictable than school. Structures are routines are essential. Students need to understand how the classroom works.

Reveal reasons. Language is so essential in working with children. Providing a rationale for a direction is important. For example, instead of saying "Stop" when a child is running in a classroom, you might say, "We need to walk in the classroom so that everyone stays safe."

Discussion Questions

Working in an inclusive preschool classroom is challenging both physically and emotionally. In order to meet the needs of young children, you must be emotionally available to each of them and vigilant in terms of the way the class on the whole is functioning. As you view this case, consider these questions:

1. There are two assistants in this classroom. Observe both Jane and the assistants. What are the key differences between the efforts of the teacher and the assistants?

2. How does Jane speak with the children both verbally and nonverbally?

3. How are challenging behaviors dealt with?

4. When Jane interacts with a student regarding his or her behavior, she provides a rationale. Give an example.

5. What are some routines in place in this classroom?

Reflections

1. Imagine yourself in a classroom full of active children. When you look around and listen to the activity you become aware of the noise level. Suddenly you wonder if other teachers or the principle thinks your classroom is out of control. How would you explain your classroom environment and its sounds to an outsider?

2. Teachers need to step back on a regular basis and consider their classroom from various perspectives. They enter a discourse with themselves. How would you structure such reflection to make sure it happened for you on a regular basis?

3. Today's classroom are multicultural and yet we ourselves are from particular cultures. The way we were taught—the many years that we observed our teachers doing things—has made a profound impression on us. How do we as professionals exercise what Harry (1999) calls cultural reciprocity? How do teachers become explicitly conscious of the values that drive their practice and allow those values to be shared with the cultural values of those individuals and families represented in our classrooms?

Case 2: Sixth Grade Social Studies

Teachers often express a concern of "losing" students with disabilities in the content areas. They are worried about students' reading levels, their writing skills, or their ability to understand complex concepts. As a result, the instruction for students with disabilities may be watered down to the extent that it is no longer interesting. With boredom and inattention come behavior problems.

This case clearly demonstrates Brophy's (1987) suggestion that a well-managed and well-structured classroom facilitates learning. Brophy suggests that monitoring the difficulty and relevance of the instruction is key. In an inclusive classroom, it is essential that all students feel as if they belong, that they are welcome, and part of the group. Because the focus is on the tasks rather than the egos involved, collaboration and ensuring the success of everyone become important. There are several ways to support this positive climate in inclusive classrooms. Here are some of the strategies that you are seeing.

Affirmation. We all need affirmation every now and then. A teacher's statement, "I know this is hard and you're working at it" can support a student struggling with a task or activity. An affirmation can help students cross the hurdle of learning a new task or behavior.

Direct appeals. Wouldn't management be easy if students followed a rule or routine just because we asked? What's interesting is that if the teacher has a strong positive relationship with his or her students, he or she can do just that. Students can be asked personally to help everyone else by curbing their enthusiasm; waiting until something is completed to speak, and so on.

Teacher proximity. The recognition of the importance of teaching proximity goes all the way back to Fritz Redl's work in the early 1950s. Moving towards students when there are indicators that something is amiss may require teaching insight but is far easier than intervening once a disruption is occurring.

Statements to promote acceptance. Reminding students about strengths and weaknesses can promote acceptance. Making statements such as "everyone can contribute something" and "some of us may be better writers, some of us may be better at drawing" helps students understand that all students contribute to the good of the classroom.

Increasing interest. Make it interesting. Although it may seem difficult, there are ways to increase task interest. Relate the content to something in the students' lives. Allow them different ways to respond. Help them see why what they are learning is important. Provide them with choices. All of these can help increase students' effort.

Clear expectations. Students do better if they know what's going to happen. Expectations can be as simple as a reminder of the routine or what you expect to accomplish in a lesson. For students for whom task completion is difficult, knowing what is expected to be accomplished can be a relief.

Positive peer support. Peer assistance can be so natural. Can't you remember a time from you own school experience when your teacher asked a peer to show you the place?

Careful reprimands. Having a positive classroom environment doesn't mean that you are prevented from reprimanding students. Look at reprimands as feedback. Sometimes you have to tell students that their behavior violates a class rule. Reprimands have to be used very carefully. Kerr and Nelson have great set of recommendations about reprimands including: (a) keep them private; (b) stand near the student you are reprimanding; (c) use a normal tone of voice; (e) look at the student, but don't require reciprocal eye contact; (f) allow the student to save face, even if that means you walk away without having the last word.

Discussion Questions

This case demonstrates a strong, positive classroom climate. But this climate didn't just happen. Sally worked hard to establish a setting in which there is mutual respect, engagement, and enthusiasm for learning. As you view this case, consider on the following questions:

1. What are some words and actions Sally uses that communicate her positive feelings towards the students?

2. The students report back about vocabulary words that they heard used over the weekend. What does this tell you about student engagement?

3. Is there a "front" to this classroom"? What does this communicate to the students? How does Sally prevent the sense of a front and back of the classroom?

4. How are students given ownership in this classroom?

5. Can you identify the reprimand that occurs? What are the characteristics of this reprimand?

Reflections

1. Setting up desk and chair arrangements is such an easy thing to do, yet this teacher has transformed this mundane task into a vehicle of ownership and responsibility for children. What can you do in your environment that would send clear messages to your students that this classroom is their classroom?

2. Whether it is a lesson about the ancient pyramids or the construction of the Empire State Building, a curricular topic can be organized and seen from several

angles. The instructor can integrate writing, mathematics, and social studies into lessons. What are your strengths or areas of needed growth in the curriculum and how will that influence your planning and level of curricular integration?

3. One of the core values of this teacher is respect for the learner. She operationalized this respect in her approach to children. Gentle reprimands were given in the hallway and a slight touch on the shoulder brought a child back to focus on a project. She listened to children's need for control of the environment, and provided earned incentives. Consider one of your core values that drive your practice. How would an observer know this value was important to you? What would the observer see you doing or hear children saying to become aware that this key value was operative in your classroom?

Case 3: Middle School Team Meeting

Assessment is a team effort and drives planning. Identifying what a child can do in a content area assists the planning of the next proximal steps of development. Maintaining high standards and multifaceted instruction creates reachable expectations through various approaches and modes of learning.

Starting with strengths. Difficult behaviors are frequently rooted in the students' experiences of the academic environment, its methods, and the students' level of success. A functional assessment of behaviors and academic performance will illuminate possible paths for instructional focus. It's easy to start with the negative. Beginning with strengths shifts the whole discussion about a student.

Identify concerns. Critical to achieving an instructional focus is the process of gaining a deeper understanding of the children in your classroom. Generally, information about a child should be gathered from triangulated sources. Interviews with teachers about the areas of greatest concern may be helpful in targeting specific times and places to conduct direct observations of the learner. It is important to look at all the environments of the learner. Sometimes knowing where a child is not having a problem is as important as knowing where a child's problem behaviors are frequently found.

Academic inroads. Even when instruction is well-planned and interventions are effectively designed, it is important that staff be aware of situations and events that have significant impact on the child. A reinforcement that works most of the time may not be effective in the presence of a certain setting event. For example, hunger may not be significant after one has just eaten. Setting events can occur in the same environment as the behavior or independently. Identifying strengths in specific non-academic areas can lead to developing strengths in an academic area.

Context. Behaviors do not occur in vacuums. A child's behaviors and learning processes can be influenced by several factors. A systems approach will keep the team alert to such things as cultural factors, family issues, time of day, and peer relationships.

Identify goals. Setting goals is a process based in hypothesis. The hypothesis is rooted in the data collection and attempts to articulate the function of the behavior as well as a replacement behavior or approach to the learning context.

Accommodations and adaptations. Teachers understand the heart of their teaching lessons and are the most qualified to understand how to create alternate approaches to the materials, when necessary.

Challenges to implementation and follow-up. Evaluation is ongoing in the process. Scaffolding may need to be increased or reduced. The hypothesis may have been off and the team may need to readjust their teaching strategies. Another critical aspect of design is the follow-up procedure. The team sets target dates to check in and continues to evaluate effectiveness. Students are involved in the assessment of their own behaviors. They are encouraged to self-monitor and well as to participate in the process of uncovering motivations and possible solutions to challenging situations. Participation and voice are empowering behaviors.

Discussion Questions

In this team meeting, a young man at risk for failing is discussed. Remarkably, he is described in very positive terms, and the emphasis is on helping rather than excluding. As you view this case, consider these questions:

1. The student being discussed is described as vulnerable. How is he vulnerable?

2. Why is a "C" a more appropriate goal than an "A"?

3. What is the purpose of this team meeting?

4. What is the impact of beginning with strengths? Is this typical of a problem-solving meeting?

5. What active listening skills do you see Steve (the facilitator) using?

Reflections

1. Meetings such as this are time intensive. Time is one of the most precious commodities a teacher has. If you have 135 students in your classroom, how can you devote such critical amounts of time to an individual? What happens if you ignore such needs?

2. This team met with the parent and the child the previous day to discuss various issues. Based on their conversation can you describe several advantages of having the child present in such a meeting? Do you think the parent felt like he or she was an integral part of this team's proceedings?

3. Besides the curricular issues that were referred to in this team meeting, what were other key concerns that these teachers were addressing as integral for this student's growth? How would you develop a process of reflection among cooperative teachers to make sure you had time to address such concerns?

Case 4: High School Physics

One challenge in inclusive schools is that of limiting students' class choices to those in which they can fully participate. For some students, there could be very few selections. This brings us to the idea of partial participation, which involves assisting students to participate in classes to the level they are able, making sure that they are viewed as true members of the class, and ensuring that everyone responds to the best of his or her ability. Without partial participation, students with disabilities may never engage in discussion of ethics, social justice, or personal identity, because these topics may be deemed "beyond them."

Addressing multiple goals. If we have students who are participating at different levels, we have to know what we want them to accomplish. Sometimes the goal may be just to be socially interacting with students without identified disabilities. Sometimes the goal may not be apparent—rather than a goal of accomplishing the content, the goal may be related to using language, requesting help, managing attention, or some other social or behavioral need.

Multilevel assignments. In providing multilevel assignments, it's important to reiterate that fair does not mean equal treatment. How can it be fair for a student for whom writing is a significant challenge to have to produce a written product on the same level as his or her peers? Concrete examples, or pictures may be needed. More time may be required. Alternative ways of responding may need to be developed.

Peer supports. Peers are sometimes more effective than the teacher in redirecting another student's behavior. Peers can get away with statements, reminders, and cues, that teachers cannot. Think of a student who is not participating in his or her group. The group has a task that needs to be completed. What would be more effective—the teacher saying "get to work," or a peer saying, "stop goofing off—we need to finish this"? Peers can focus on tasks just as teachers can in terms of redirecting behavior.

Empowering students. By the time students are adolescents, they need to be able to identify when they need help. Rather than doing something for the student, the teacher's question becomes, "How can I help you with this?" Intervening with students is not the same as doing for them. Students begin to recognize their strengths and weaknesses and communicate their needs.

Self-advocacy. Students can be helped to establish their own goals and monitor progress. Sometimes this is as simple as asking a student what he or she intends to complete during the class time. Students can be asked what kind of help they need to complete the task.

Multilevel assessments. The question becomes, "What is the critical performance for each student that will let me know that the content is being learned at the level appropriate for each student?" The means of the evaluation becomes less important than the end. Assessment also must be ongoing—the teacher has to monitor students' comprehension constantly.

Recognizing contributions. In an inclusive classroom, everyone's contribution is valued. Reporting out should include comments made by everyone. Sometimes the contribution may be remaining quiet so others could complete work when the student is having a hard day. In an inclusive classroom each individual's contribution is essential to completing the goals of the class.

Involving students. Participation can be supported at the simplest level by teacher encouragement. Praising effort also becomes essential. Success or failure is attributed to things within the students' control.

Discussion Questions

Students with special needs are often excluded from what is considered "higher level classes." Yet in this classroom, a diverse group of students are highly engaged in a complex physics activity. As you view this case, consider these questions:

1. How does the teacher communicate that each student's contribution is valued?

2. How do the students demonstrate ownership?

3. How do the students support each other?

4. How does the teacher bring physics to life for the students?

Reflections

1. Providing a safe environment, physically and psychologically, is a significant part of preparing a learning environment. Everyone had a hard hat and a reflective vest on the construction work site. The classroom was arranged for easy access to work spaces and computers. Considering the principles of universal design, what are the priorities that you will establish to provide safety and security in your learning environment?

2. Once a collaborative learning environment is created, peer assistance, such as think aloud and structured responses, becomes a vital and affirming practice for learners (Fuchs, 2001). Can you describe specific and structured ways to train students how to assist one another? What are the risks involved in peer assistance issues? What qualities must a teacher have to make this learning dynamic successful?

3. Developmentally, children require increasing levels of control. Choice is a way to provide this power to learners (Kohn, 1993). How was choice exercised in this classroom? Can you brainstorm a variety of meaningful choices for learners in a project you might design for a classroom of high school students?

Performance Assessment Probes

Each of the following performance assessment probes provide evidence for the indicated Council for Exceptional Children standard. We hope responding to these probes will assist you, the student, in constructing knowledge about inclusive classrooms.

Performance Assessment Probe 1

Council for Exceptional Children Standard 1: Foundations

Task: Generate a one- to two-page narrative that:
- describes the principle of normalization
- provides specific examples from one or more cases that illustrate examples of normalization

Rubric for Assessment

Rating → / Content ↓	Unacceptable 1	Basic 2	Proficient 3	Outstanding 4
Defines concept	Inaccurate or missing definition	Superficial understanding; copies words from text	Demonstrates understanding of the concept	Demonstrates understanding of the concept and provides related literature
Exemplars	Missing or misidentified examples	One or two obvious examples	Three or more examples analyzed and contrasted	Four or more examples analyzed and contrasted
Clarity and organization	Rambling; single paragraph; grammatical/spelling errors	Simple essay format	Essay format, clear advance organizer and summary	Integrated analysis

Performance Assessment Probe 2

Council for Exceptional Children Standard 4: Instructional Strategies
Council for Exceptional Children Standard 5: Learning Environments and Social Interactions
INTASC Principle 5: The teacher uses an understanding of individual and group motivation and behavior to create a learning environment that encourages positive social interaction, active engagement in learning, and self-motivation.

Task: Choose on of the three classroom cases. Analyze the instructional strategies used by the teacher and the ways in which these strategies also support the classroom climate.

Rubric for Assessment

Rating ➔ Content ⬇	Unacceptable 1	Basic 2	Proficient 3	Outstanding 4
Provides context for narrative	Not provided	Simple context provided	Multilevel description of context	Detailed description of context
Exemplars	Missing or misidentified examples	One or two obvious examples	Three or more examples analyzed and contrasted	Four or more examples analyzed and contrasted
Clarity and organization	Rambling; single paragraph; grammatical/spelling errors	Simple essay format	Essay format, clear advance organizer and summary	Integrated analysis
Analysis	No analysis; lists	Simple analysis	Analyzes and contrasts learning strategies and climate	Detailed analysis and integration of description of strategies and climate

Performance Assessment Probe 3

Council for Exceptional Children Standard 10: Collaboration
INTASC Principle 10: The teacher fosters relationships with school colleagues, parents, and agencies in the larger community to support students' learning and well-being.

Task: View the team meeting case. In terms of Pugach and Johnson's (1995) description of active listening skills, analyze the interactions that take place. Provide examples of listening skills, and describe the impact they have on the interaction.

Rubric for Assessment

Rating → Content ↓	Unacceptable 1	Basic 2	Proficient 3	Outstanding 4
Provide context for discussion	No context	Superficial understanding; copies words from text	Demonstrates understanding of the concept	Demonstrates understanding of the concept and provides related literature
Exemplars	Missing or misidentified examples	One or two obvious examples	Three or more examples analyzed and contrasted	Four or more examples analyzed and contrasted
Clarity and organization	Rambling; single paragraph; grammatical/spelling errors	Simple essay format	Essay format, clear advance organizer and summary	Integrated analysis

Performance Assessment Probe 4

Council for Exceptional Children Standard 9: Professional and Ethical Practice

Task: Lipson and Wixson (1997) suggest that the most influential factor in the instructional setting is the teacher's knowledge and beliefs about teaching and learning. We all have our own belief system from which we teach. Listen to the voices of the teachers in the Preschool, Sixth Grade, and High School cases. Describe the common threads in their beliefs about teaching and learning. Then describe your own stance, providing examples about your desired classroom climate, general goals for your classroom, and beliefs about students with disabilities.

Rubric for Assessment

Rating➔ Content⬇	Unacceptable 1	Basic 2	Proficient 3	Outstanding 4
Clarity and accuracy of presentation	Unclear; inaccurate; rambling	Presentation is understandable; contains few errors	Presentation easy to understand; no errors	Well-written, articulate presentation
Common threads among teachers	Fails to identify commonalities	Few, simple commonalities identified	Several commonalities explored and contrasted	Commonalities explored and summarized by clearly communicated themes
Description of personal stance: Climate	Missing, unclear	Few, basic, clear statements	Clear statements of belief statement	Articulate, reflective, theory-grounded statements
General goals for classroom	Missing, unclear	Few, basic, clear statements	Clear statements of belief statement	Articulate, reflective, theory-grounded statements
Beliefs about students with disabilities	Missing, unclear	Few, basic, clear statements	Clear statements of belief statement	Articulate, reflective, theory-grounded statements
Written communication	Stereotypical language; many grammatical errors; poor presentation	Simple language; some errors; basic presentation	Person-first, respectful language; no errors	Reflective, respectful language, no errors; creatively presented

Performance Assessment Probe 5

Council for Exceptional Children Standard 5: Learning Environments and Social Interactions

Task: Review the three classroom cases. Generate a chart in which you provide exemplars of each of these general considerations of inclusive settings:
- Teacher reflection
- Flexibility
- Individualization
- Caring
- Natural supports
- Fairness

Rubric for Assessment

Rating→ Content↓	Unacceptable 1	Basic 2	Proficient 3	Outstanding 4
Format	Not presented as chart	Presented as chart; single examples only	Presented in chart; more than one example in several areas	Presented in chart; several examples in each area
Accuracy	Several missing items or inaccurately identified items	Few inaccurately identified items	No inaccurately identified items	Items accurately identified and explained
Presentation	Confusing; unclear	Clear communication, few grammatical errors	No grammatical errors; clear communication	Compelling arguments; no errors

Performance Assessment Probe 6

Council for Exceptional Children Standard 4: Instructional Strategies

Task: Rose and Meyer (2000) suggest that Universal Design is grounded in (a) multiple, flexible methods of presentation used to support diverse recognition networks; (b) multiple flexible methods of expression; and (c) multiple, flexible methods of engagement. Reflect on a classroom that you have recently observed, or, if necessary, one of your current classes. Provide examples (or counter examples) to each of these indicators of Universal Design. This should be completed in a written narrative.

Rubric for Assessment

Rating➜ Content⬇	Unacceptable 1	Basic 2	Proficient 3	Outstanding 4
Clarity and accuracy of presentation	Unclear; inaccurate; rambling	Presentation is understandable; contains few errors	Presentation easy to understand; no errors	Well-written, articulate presentation
Indicators	Missing indicator(s)	One, simple example or counter example	Two or three examples or counter examples; explanation	Several indicators; complex discussion
Presentation	Confusing; unclear	Clear communication, few grammatical errors	No grammatical errors; clear communication	Compelling arguments; no errors
Accuracy	Several missing items or inaccurately identified items	Few inaccurately identified items	No inaccurately identified items	Items accurately identified and explained
Summarization and reflection	No summarization or reflection	Simple summarization	Summarization and reflection	Insightful summarization and reflection

Performance Assessment Probe 7

Council for Exceptional Children Standard 4: Instructional Strategies

Task: There are three elements of differentiated instruction: content, process, and product (Tomlinson, 2001). Review either the Sixth Grade or High School case. Identify various ways in which content, process, or product are differentiated for the students who vary from their peers. Using your own experience, describe a hypothetical lesson and the ways in which you would adjust content, process, or product. This should be completed in a written narrative.

Rubric for Assessment

Rating➜ Content⬇	Unacceptable 1	Basic 2	Proficient 3	Outstanding 4
Clarity and accuracy of presentation	Unclear; inaccurate; rambling	Presentation is understandable; contains few errors	Presentation easy to understand; no errors	Well-written, articulate presentation
Indicators	Missing indicator(s)	One, simple example or counter example	Two or three examples or counter examples; explanation	Several indicators; complex discussion
Presentation	Confusing; unclear	Clear communication, few grammatical errors	No grammatical errors; clear communication	Compelling arguments; no errors
Accuracy	Several missing items or inaccurately identified items	Few inaccurately identified items	No inaccurately identified items	Items accurately identified and explained
Summarization and reflection	No summarization or reflection	Simple summarization	Summarization and reflection	Insightful summarization and reflection

Performance Assessment Probe 8

Council for Exceptional Children Standard 8: Assessment

Task: In the Middle School Team Meeting case, the student's developmental context and setting events are identified. What aspects of his social system have an impact on his performance in school? What aspects of his setting events could be having an impact on his behavior? Describe a student with whom you have worked (or, if necessary, a hypothetical student) who is demonstrating an instructional and/or behavioral concern. In a written narrative, identify aspects within the social system and setting events that may have an impact on that concern.

Rubric for Assessment

Rating➡️ Content⬇️	Unacceptable 1	Basic 2	Proficient 3	Outstanding 4
Clarity and accuracy of presentation	Unclear; inaccurate; rambling	Presentation is understandable; contains few errors	Presentation easy to understand; no errors	Well-written, articulate presentation
Presentation	Confusing; unclear	Clear communication, few grammatical errors	No grammatical errors; clear communication	Compelling arguments; no errors
Systems related to case	No identification of systems	Response demonstrates simple understanding of social systems	Response demonstrates student recognizes various aspects of social systems	Response indicates student recognizes complex interaction of social systems
Setting events related to case	Fails to identify setting events	Identifies single or simple setting event	Identifies several appropriate setting events	Identifies setting events; provides analysis of impact
System related to generated example	No identification of systems	Response demonstrates simple understanding of social systems	Response demonstrates student recognizes various aspects of social systems	Response indicates student recognizes complex interaction of social systems
Setting events related to generated example	Fails to identify setting events	Identifies single or simple setting event	Identifies several appropriate setting events	Identifies setting events; provides analysis of impact

Performance Assessment Probe 9

Council for Exceptional Children Standard 4: Instructional Strategies

Task: In an inclusive classroom, a teacher has multiple goals for a single lesson. The goals may be related to individualized social or academic goals for each student and for the class on the whole. In the high school physics classroom, the teacher is working towards several goals. In a written narrative identify several of these potential goals and describe whether they are individual or classwide goals. Then, propose a lesson on a topic with which you are familiar in another content area. Briefly describe the lesson topic and the classroom context including age, culture, and special needs of the students. What are various goals you could have for this lesson in an inclusive classroom?

Rubric for Assessment

Rating→ Content↓	Unacceptable 1	Basic 2	Proficient 3	Outstanding 4
Clarity and accuracy of presentation	Unclear; inaccurate; rambling	Presentation is understandable; contains few errors	Presentation easy to understand; no errors	Well-written, articulate presentation
Presentation	Confusing; unclear	Clear communication, few grammatical errors	No grammatical errors; clear communication	Compelling arguments; no errors
Identification of goals	Unable to identify multiple goals	Simple identification of social and academic goals	Identification of multiple social and academic goals	Identification of multiple social and academic goals and their interaction
Description of topic and classroom context	Unclear or missing	Simple description	Clear identification of topic and classroom context	Detailed description of topic and classroom context
Identification of goals	Unable to identify multiple goals	Simple identification of social and academic goals	Identification of multiple social and academic goals	Identification of multiple social and academic goals and their interaction
Summarization and reflection	No summarization or reflection	Simple summarization	Summarization and reflection	Insightful summarization and reflection

FAQ's of Teaching in Inclusive Classrooms

Isn't inclusion just another word for mainstreaming?

Mainstreaming does not occur in any of the special education laws. Typically, however, when Public Law 94-142, the Education for All Handicapped Children Act was passed, mainstreaming referred to students being in classrooms with students with disabilities part of the time, and with students without disabilities part of the time. This usually meant students were either "pulled out" of the special education classroom for socialization or "pulled out" of the general education classroom for extra help. Mainstreamed students were not considered to be a real part of the general education classroom. They were "special." Often mainstreamed students had to "earn" the right to eat lunch in the cafeteria with everyone else, go to music or art, or to be outside for recess with their typical peers.

Does the law require inclusion?

The law requires that every student with a disability be educated in the least restrictive environment. The least restrictive environment is determined at the students' Individualized Educational Planning meeting. In the latest amendments, Public Law 105-17: The IDEA Amendments of 1997, several provisions require that those who work with individuals with disabilities have high expectations for them, document their achievement, and ensure that they have as much access to the general education curriculum as possible. The general education teacher is now a member of the IEP team. Students are assumed to be best served in the general education curriculum unless they have specific needs making such a placement inappropriate.

Don't students with disabilities do better getting more specialized help all day?

In answering this question, we have to report that in terms of research about academic performance, the verdict is still out. Students with less significant disabilities may do better than their peers with more significant disabilities (Klingner, Vaughn, Hughes, Schumm, & Elbaum, 1998). Students with disabilities, however, may demonstrate improved standardized test scores, reading performance, on-task behavior, and motivation when in general education classrooms (Waldron & McLeskey, 1998). Students themselves have indicated that they believe that the general education classroom is best for meeting their academic and social needs, and are concerned about what happens in the room if they are pulled out for special help (Vaughn & Klingner, 1998).

I'm not a special educator. How am I supposed to know what to do with these kids?

Each student with a disability has an Individualized Education Program. This program is developed collaboratively with special educators, the general educator who will serve the student, parents, and administrators. Not only are the goals and objectives for each student clearly defined, support from special educators and related services personnel usually follows the student.

What are the other services the student could receive?

Students with disabilities may receive consultative or direct services in occupational therapy, speech therapy, audiology, physical therapy, parent education, and transition services.

Aren't a lot of the things we're told to do in inclusive classrooms just good teaching?

Absolutely. Many of the teaching behaviors that are identified for students with disabilities are actually good teaching behaviors. These include all of the teacher behaviors that you have viewed in these cases.

Won't the more capable students suffer if I have a student with a disability in my class?

Students with no identified disabilities in inclusive classrooms have not been found to receive less instruction (Hollowood, Salisbury, Rainforth & Palombaro, 1994) or have lower achievement (Saint-Laurent et al., 1998).

If everyone is working and everyone is learning, don't you forget who has disabilities and who doesn't?

That's the idea behind using differentiated instruction and Universal Design for Learning. There are no "typical" students; each has his or her own unique strengths and needs. Through using these techniques, all children have an increased potential for achieving.

I have never had students with disabilities in my classroom before, and now I do! Where do I start in making my classroom an inclusive classroom?

Janney and Snell (1997) talk about two kinds of changes that have to occur in the transition to an inclusive classroom. First, classroom routines may need to be modified. The timing and location of activities may need to be changed, and you may need additional time to transition from one activity to another. Second, modifications may need to be made in your instructional activities. Students may need to have academic adaptations, in which they are socially participating in the goals of the class lesson with some support to meet their individualized learning goals. They may be engaging in social participation strategies, in which you are trying to incorporate them into the community of the classroom. Or, they may actually be engaged in parallel activities, in which students are completing a variation of the activities that the other members of the class are completing.

Why do I need to be at the IEP meeting?

You need to be at the IEP meeting for several reasons. First, the federal regulations state that the general education teacher is a member of the IEP team. Second, if you are going to be participating in the education of a student with disabilities and providing some of the instruction, it is critical that you have input into the goals of that instruction. This is your opportunity to speak on behalf of the child. You have information about the child's functioning in your classroom that is unique and essential.

Why do we do IEPs?

The IEP serves many purposes. IEPs provide (NICHCY, 1990):
- Communication tools that provide a way for parents and school personnel to work together to identify students' needs, the services that are needed to meet those needs, and the anticipated outcomes.
- Opportunities for resolving differences between parents and the school.
- A commitment of resources necessary to enable students to receive needed special education and related services.
- A way of ensuring that students receive the special education and related services they require.
- A means of monitoring whether students are actually receiving the free, appropriate, public education on which the parents and school have agreed.
- An evaluation tool to determine the extent of the student's progress toward the projected goals and objectives.

In addition, the IEP clarifies the students' role in statewide assessments and documents technological aids needed.

Sample Responses to Case Discussion Questions

Case 1: Preschool Classroom

1. There are two assistants in this classroom. Observe both Jane and the assistants. What are the key differences between the efforts of the teacher and the assistants?
    *   Jane is constantly vigilant regarding all of the activities in the classroom, scanning and interacting.
    *   Though Jane interacts with individual children, rather than engaging in extended interactions, she seems to go where needed.

2. How does Jane speak with the children both verbally and nonverbally?
    *   Gets down on their level
    *   Makes eye contact
    *   Smiles
    *   Appears affirming (nods, smiles, looks interested)
    *   Asks questions to expand interaction

3. How are challenging behaviors dealt with?
    *   Students are redirected.
    *   Students are given a rationale regarding the need to change their behavior.
    *   Students are supported rather than chastised.
    *   Students are given a safe outlet.

4. When Jane interacts with a student regarding his or her behavior, she provides a rationale. Give an example.
    *   Keeping the beans in the sand table.

5. What are some routines in place in this classroom?
    *   Put things back after playing with them.
    *   The number of students at each activity managed by the chairs or materials available.

Case 2: Sixth Grade

1. What are some words and actions Sally uses that communicates her positive feelings towards the students?
    *   Welcomes students back.
    *   Welcomes a student specifically by name.
    *   Gives student a hug and touches other student who gives her the wreath they made. (That they made her a wreath is in itself significant.)
    *   Recognizes student achievement out of school.
    *   Recognizes that students have been out of school for four days and remembering is difficult.

2.   The students report back about vocabulary words that they heard used over the weekend. What does this tell you about student engagement?
   • Students are thinking about language arts content when they aren't in school; students are interested and engaged

3.   Is there a "front" to this classroom"? What does this communicate to the students? How does Sally prevent the sense of a front and back of the classroom?
   • There is no "front"—much of the review is conducted from what would be considered the side of the room
   • Lack of traditional rows makes the "front" difficult to determine
   • Sally is constantly moving, making the sense of "front" and "back" irrelevant; students are all part of the whole group

4.   How are students given ownership in this classroom?
   • Class officers conduct the opening activity
   • Students are cued to make a plan
   • Activity requires students to think about what they would include as their most prized possessions

5.   Can you identify the reprimand that occurs? What are the characteristics of this reprimand?
   • A student is reading a comic book. The teacher approaches the student quietly and privately, and asks him to participate in a way that draws little if no attention.

Case 3: Middle School Team

1.   The student being discussed is described as vulnerable. How is he vulnerable?
   • If what is happening for this student is not changed, he will fail.

2.   Why is a "C" a more appropriate goal than an "A"?
   • When a student is failing, an "A" is completely out of reach. A "C" is a much more appropriate goal.

3.   What is the purpose of this team meeting?
   • To find ways to support this student. The emphasis is on changing what the teachers are doing, not changing the student.

4.   What is the impact of beginning with strengths? Is this typical of a problem solving meeting?
   • Beginning with strengths changes the emphasis on the meeting from changing the child to using the strengths to increase the likelihood of his success.

5. What active listening skills do you see Steve (the facilitator) using?

- Offering support
- Using general, nonthreatening openings.
- Restating what another individual contributed to make sure the information is clear.
- Verbalizing the message you feel is being implied.
- Asking the speaker to clarify.
- Allowing silence to occur so that participants can reflect.
- Putting events in the proper order and context.
- Summarizing so that everyone has an opportunity to agree or disagree with what was said.

Case 4: High School

1. How does the teacher communicate that each student's contribution is valued?
   - Explicitly states, "Some of you will be _____. Some of you will be _____."

2. How do the students demonstrate ownership?
   - Giving examples that are real to them (football).
   - Volunteering to complete parts of the task.

3. How do the students support each other?
   - Rewording the task.
   - Explaining.
   - Praising.
   - Providing students with tasks with which they will be successful.

4. How does the teacher bring physics to life for the students?
   - Taking the students to the construction site;
   - requiring that they go beyond the book;
   - relating concepts to football.

Index to Video Cases and Related Chapter Topics

In this index we cross-reference topics presented in the video cases with the related chapter topics from *The Inclusive Classroom: Strategies for Effective Instruction*, Second Edition, by Margo A. Mastropieri and Thomas E. Scruggs.

Topic	Video Case	Relevant Chapter(s) and Section(s)
Assessment	Middle School	Chapter 12: Assessment
Assessment, behavioral disorders	Middle School	Chapter 7: Managing Classroom Behavior
Assessment, functional behavioral	Middle School	Chapter 12: Assessment
Attention	Sixth Grade	Chapter 10: Attention
Behavior management, principles	Preschool; Middle School	Chapter 7: Managing Classroom Behavior
Behavior management, strategies	Preschool; Middle School	Chapter 7: Managing Classroom Behavior
Choice	Sixth Grade	Chapter 9, Techniques for Improving Motivation and Affect
Classroom climate	Sixth Grade	Chapter 9, Techniques for Improving Motivation and Affect
Classroom management	Middle School	Chapter 7: Managing Classroom Behavior
Collaboration, assessment	Middle School	Chapter 2: Collaboration to Establish Need
Collaboration, teaming	Middle School	Chapter 2: Collaboration to Establish Need
Content-area instruction	High School	Chapters 13 through 16
Cooperative learning	High School	Chapter 8, Cooperative Learning
Effective instruction	Sixth Grade; High School	Chapter 6, Overview of Effective Instruction
Empowerment	Sixth Grade; High School	Chapter 9, Preconditions for Improving Motivation and Affect
Encouragement	Middle School,	Chapter 9, Preconditions for Improving Motivation and Affect
Engagement	Sixth Grade; High School	Chapter 6, Overview of Effective Instruction
Expectations	Sixth Grade; High School	Chapter 9, Preconditions for Improving Motivation and Affect
Explicitness	Sixth Grade; High School	Chapter 9, Preconditions for Improving Motivation and Affect
Feedback	All Cases	Chapter 9, Preconditions for Improving Motivation and Affect
Flexibility	Sixth Grade; High School	Chapter 9, Preconditions for Improving Motivation and Affect
Functional behavioral assessment	Middle School	Chapter 12: Assessment

Grouping	High School	Chapter 9, Preconditions for Improving Motivation and Affect
Objectives, instructional	High School	Chapter 6, Planning for Content Coverage
Organizational skills	Middle School	Chapter 11, Tools to Develop Independent Learner
Parents	Middle School	Chapter 3, Mental Retardation
Peers	High School; Middle School	Chapter 8, Peer Assistance
Reprimands	Sixth Grade	Chapter 7, Managing Classroom Behavior
Self-management	All Cases	Chapter 7: Managing Classroom Behavior
Social needs	Preschool; Middle School	Chapter 7: Managing Classroom Behavior

References

(recommended as additional readings)

Apter, S. J., & Propper, C. A. (1986). Ecological perspectives on youth violence. In S. J. Apter & A. P. Goldstein (Eds.), *Youth violence: Programs and prospects* (pp. 160–159). New York: Pergamon Press.

Bambara, L. M., & Mitchell-Kvacky, N. A. &1994). Positive behavior support for students with severe disabilities: An emerging multicomponent approach for addressing challenging behaviors. *School Psychology Review, 23*(2), 263–278.

Birch, S. H., & Ladd, G. W. (1998). Children's interpersonal behaviors and the teacher-child relationship. *Developmental Psychology, 35,* 61–80.

Bishop, K. D., & Jubala, K. A. (1995). Positive behavior support strategies. In M. A. Farley (Ed.), *Inclusive and heterogeneous schooling: Assessment, curriculum, and instruction* (pp. 159–186). Baltimore: Paul H. Brookes.

Block, M. E. (1994). *A teacher's guide to including students with disabilities in regular physical education.* Baltimore: Paul H. Brooks.

Bronfenbrenner, U. (1986). Ecology of the family as a context for human development: Research perspectives. *Developmental Psychology, 22*(6), 723–742.

Calderhead, J. (1996). Teachers: Beliefs and knowledge. In D. C. Berliner & R. C. Calfee (Eds.), *Handbook of educational psychology* (pp. 709–725). New York: Macmillan

Chow, P., Blais, L., & Hemingway, J. (1999). An outsider looking in: Total inclusion and the concept of equifinality. *Education, 119*(3), 459–464.

Dadson, S., & Horner, R. H. (1993). Manipulating setting events to decrease problem behaviors: A case study. *Teaching Exceptional Children, 25*(3), 53–58.

Daniels, V. I. (1998). How to manage disruptive behavior in inclusive classrooms. *Teaching Exceptional Children, 30*(4), 26–31.

Evans, I., & Meyer, L. (1985). *Educative approach to behavior problems: A practical decision model for interventions with severely handicapped learners.* Baltimore, MD: Paul H. Brookes.

Ford, A., Davern, L., & Schnorr, R. (20001). Learners with significant disabilities: Curricular relevance in an era of standards-based reform. *Remedial and Special Education, 22*(4), 214–222.

Fuchs, L. S., & Fuchs, D. (2001). Principles for prevention and intervention of mathematics difficulties. *Learning Disabilities Research and Practice, 16*(2), 85–95.

Good, T. L., & Brophy, J. (1995). *Contemporary educational psychology* (5th ed.). Reading, MA: Addison Wesley Longman.

Gore, J. M., & Zeichner, K. M. (1991). Action research and reflective teaching in preservice teacher education: A case study from the United States. *Teaching and Teacher Education, 7*(2), 119–136.

Guild, P. (1994). The culture/learning style connection. *Educational Leadership*, May, 16–21.

Harry, B. (1999). Cultural reciprocity in sociocultural perspective: Adapting the normalization principle for family collaboration. *Exceptional Children, 66*(1), 123–136.

Hayek, R. A. (1987). The teacher assistance team: A prereferral support system. *Focus on Exceptional Children, 20*(1), 1–7.

Hildebrand, V., & Hearron, P. (1999). *Guiding young children.* Upper Saddle River, NJ: Prentice Hall.

Hindin, A., Morocco, C. C., & Aguilar, C. M. (2001). "This book lives in our school;" Teaching middle school students to understand literature. *Remedial and Special Education, 22*(4), 204–213.

Hollowood, T. M., Salisbury, C. L., Rainforth, B., & Palombaro, M. M. (1994). Use of instructional time in classrooms serving students with and without severe disabilities. *Exceptional Children, 61*(3), 242–253.

Horner, R. H., Vaughn, B. J., Day, H. M., & Ard, W. R. (1996). The relationship between setting events and problem behavior. In S. K. Koegel, R. L. Koegel, & G. Dunlap (Eds.), *Positive behavior support: Including people with difficult behaviors in the community* (pp. 381–402). Baltimore: Paul H. Brookes.

Hoy, W. K., & Woolfolk, A. E. (1990). Socialization of student teachers. *American Educational Research Journal, 27*, 279–300.

Jackson, R., & Harper, K. (2002). *Teacher planning and the universal design for learning.* Wakefield, MA: National Center on Accessing the General Curriculum.

Jackson, R., Harper, K., & Jackson, J. (2002*). Effective teaching practices and their barriers limiting their use in accessing the curriculum: A review of recent* *literature*. Wakefield, MA: National Center on Accessing the General Curriculum.

Janney, R. E., & Snell, M. E. (1997). How teachers include students with moderate and severe disabilities in elementary classes: The means and meaning of inclusion. *Journal of the Association for Persons with Severe Handicaps, 22*(3), 159–169.

Jenkins, J. R., Pious, C. G., & Jewell, M. (1990). Special education and the regular education initiative: Basic assumptions. *Exceptional Children, 56*, 479–491.

Kagen, D. M. (1992). Professional growth among preservice and beginning teachers. *Review of Educational Research, 62,* 129–169.

Kennedy, C. H., & Itkonen, T. (1993). Effects of setting events on the problem behavior of students with severe disabilities. *Journal of Applied Behavior Analysis, 26*(3), 321–327.

Klingner, J. K., Vaughn, S., Hughes, M. T., Schumm, J. S., & Elbaum, B. (1998). Outcomes for students with and without learning disabilities in inclusive classrooms. *Learning Disabilities Research and Practice, 13*(3), 153–161.

Kohn, A. (1993). *Punished by rewards: the trouble with gold stars, incentive plans, A's, praise, and other bribes.* New York: Houghton Mifflin

Lipsky, D. K., & Gartner, A. (1991). Achieving full inclusion: Placing the student at the center of educational reform. In W. Stainback & S. Stainback, (Eds.), *Controversial issues confronting special education: Divergent perspectives* (pp. 3–12). Needham Heights, MA: Allyn & Bacon.

Lipson, M. Y., & Wixson, K. K. (1997). *Assessment and instruction of reading and writing disability*. New York: Longman.

Long, N., Morse, W. C., & Newman, R. G. (1980). *Conflict in the classroom: The education of emotionally disturbed children* (4th ed.). Belmont, CA: Wadsworth.

Lortie, D. C. (1975). *Schoolteacher: A sociological study*. Chicago: The University of Chicago Press.

Lyon, S., & Lyon, G. (1980). Team functioning and staff development: A role release approach to providing integrated educational services to severely handicapped students. *Journal of the Association for Persons with Severe Handicaps*, 5, 250–263.

Mace, R. (1997). *The Center for Universal Design*. Retrieved on December 11, 2002, from www.design.ncsu.edu/cud/univ_design/princ_overview.htm.

Marion, M. (1999). *Guidance of young children* (5th ed.). Upper Saddle River, NJ: Prentice Hall.

Montague, M., & Rinaldi, C. (2001). Classroom dynamics and children at risk: A followup. *Learning Disabilities Quarterly, 24*(2), 75–83.

National Parent Teacher Association. (1997). *Teacher's guide to parent and family involvement.* Chicago: Author.

NICHCY (National Information Center for Children and Youth with Handicaps (1990). *Questions often asked about special education services.* Washington, DC: Author.

Nirje, B. (1967). The normalization principle and its human management implications. In R. Kugel & W. Wolfensberger (Eds.), *Changing patterns of residential services for the mentally retarded* (pp. 42–65). Washington, DC: President's Committee on Mental Retardation.

Nisbet, J. (1992). Introduction. In J. Nisbet (Ed.), *Natural supports in school, at work, and in the community for people with severe disabilities* (pp. 1-10). Baltimore: Paul H. Brookes.

Noddings, N. (1984). *Caring: A feminine approach to ethics and moral education.* Berkeley, CA: University of California Press.

Odom, S. L., & Bailey, D. (2001). Inclusive preschool programs: Classroom ecology and child outcomes (pp. 253–276). In M. J. Guralnick, Ed., *Early childhood inclusion.* Baltimore, MD: Paul H. Brookes.

Orkwis, R., & McLane, K. (1998). *A curriculum every student can use: Design principles for student access.* (ERIC-OSEP Topical Brief). Reston, VA: ERIC-OSEP Special Project, Council for Exceptional Children.

Pisha, B., & Coyne, P. (2001). Smart from the start: The promise of Universal Design for Learning. *Remedial and Special Education, 22*(4), 197–203.

Pugach, M., & Johnson, L. J. (1988). Rethinking the relationship between consultation and collaborative problem-solving. *Focus on Exceptional Children, 21*(4), 1–8.

Redl, F. (1959). The concept of the life space interview. *American Journal of Orthopsychiatry, 29*, 1–18.

Rogers, D. L., Waller, C. B., & Perrin, M. S. (1987). Learning more about what makes a good teacher through collaborative research in the classroom. *Young Children*, 34–39.

Rose, D., & Meyer, A. (2002). Universal design for individual differences. *Educational Leadership, 58*(3), 39–43.

Saint-Laurent, L., Dionne, J., Giasson, J., Royer, E., Simard, C., & Pierard, B. (1998). Academic achievement effects of an in-class service model on students with and without disabilities. *Exceptional Children, 64,* 239–253.

Salvia, J., & Ysseldyke, J. E. (1991). *Assessment in special and remedial education* (5th Ed.). Boston: Houghton Mifflin

Sapon-Shevin, M. (1990). Initial steps for developing a caring school. In W. Stainback & S. Stainback (Eds.), *Support networks for inclusive schools: Interdependent integrated education* (pp. 241–248). Baltimore: Paul H. Brookes.

Schmidt, R. J., Rozendal, M. S., & Greenman, G. G. (2002). Reading instruction in the inclusion classroom: Research-based practices. *Remedial and Special Education, 23*(3), 130–140.

Stanovich, P. J., & Jordan, A. (2002). Preparing general educators to teach in inclusive classrooms: Some food for thought. *Teacher Educator, 37*(3), 173–185.

Sugai, G., & Horner, R. H. (1994). Including students with severe behavior problems in general education setting: Assumptions, challenges, and solutions. In J. Marr, G. Sugai, & G. Tindal (Eds.), *The Oregon Conference Monograph, 6,* (pp. 109–129). Eugene, OR: University of Oregon.

Tomlinson, C. (1995). *How to differentiate instruction in mixed-ability classrooms.* Alexandria, VA: Association for Supervision and Curriculum Development.

Tomlinson, C. (2001). *How to differentiate instruction in mixed-ability classrooms* (2nd Ed.). Alexandria, VA: Association for Supervision and Curriculum Development.

Turnbull, A. H., Edmonson, H., Griggs, P., Wickham, D., Sailor, W., Freeman, R., Guess, D., Lassen, S., Mccart, A., Park, J., Riffel, L., Turnbull, R., & Warren, J. (2002). A blueprint for schoolwide positive behavior support: Implementation of three components. *Exceptional Children, 68*(3), 377–402.

Vaughn, S., & Klingner, J. K. (1998). Students' perceptions of inclusion and resource room settings. *The Journal of Special Education, 32*(2), 79–88.

Waldron, N. L., & McLeskey, J. (1998). The effects of an inclusive school program on students with mild and severe learning disabilities. *Exceptional Children, 64,* 395–405.

Weiss, J. R. (1981). Learned helplessness in black and white children identified by their schools as retarded and nonretarded. *Developmental Psychology, 17,* 499–508.

White, K. J., Jones, K., & Sherman, M. D. (1998). Reputation information and teacher feedback: Their influences on children's perceptions of behavior problem peers. *Journal of Social and Clinical Psychology, 17,* 11–37.

Zeichner, K. M., & Liston, D. P. (1987). Teaching student teachers to reflect. *Harvard Educational Review, 57*(1), 23–48.